Choose Love

A Simple Path to Healthy, Joyful Relationships

Margot Schulman

Copyright © 2019 Margot Schulman.

ALL RIGHTS RESERVED. This book contains material protected under International and Federal Copyright Laws and Treaties. Any unauthorized reprint or use of this material is prohibited. No part of this book may be reproduced or transmitted in any form or by any means, electronic or mechanical, including photocopying, recording, or by any information storage and retrieval system without express written permission from the author/publisher.

Library of Congress Control Number: 2019905588

Paperback: 978-1-64085-688-2
Hardback: 978-1-64085-689-9

DEDICATION

This book is dedicated to all my loved ones. In particular, my mom, my children - Isadora and Oliver and my sweetheart Danny. Big Love and smooches.

ACKNOWLEDGEMENTS

I wish to express my deep gratitude for all of my clients who have taught me so much. I also wish to thank all my teachers, coaches, guides and friends who have shared their light and wisdom with me. A special shout out to Lisa Wechtenhiser, Keylan Qazzaz, Melissa Henige, Danny Sherman and Layla Martin. I also wish to acknowledge my mother, Joan Schulman for her unending patience and support in editing the first draft of this book. And I bow to my other mother - Divine Mama Earth - for sharing her unwavering love, support and beauty with me every day of my life.

TABLE OF CONTENTS

Introduction 1

PART ONE:
PRACTICE PRESENCE & BUILD ACCEPTANCE

Chapter 1	Practice Presence with Yourself 9	
	Get to Know Yourself 11	
	Learn to Listen to Yourself............... 12	
	Checking in with Yourself 12	
	Advanced Check-In Tips 16	
	Declare a Truce with the Protectors 18	
	Facing Down Resistance 23	
Chapter 2	Practice Presence with Others 26	
	The Need to Be Seen................... 26	
	Holding Space........................ 28	
Chapter 3	Presence with your Children 30	
	Holding Space for Your Kids:	
	The Inner Work...................... 33	
	Holding Space for Your Kids:	
	The Outer Work 35	
Chapter 4	Presence with Parents and Siblings 37	
Chapter 5	Presence with Romantic Partners.......... 42	
Chapter 6	Constant vigilance! 48	

PART TWO:
EXPAND COMPASSION & TRUST

Chapter 7	Practicing Presence with Your Pain	53
Chapter 8	Reframing Pain	56
Chapter 9	Overcoming Shame with Integrity	60
Chapter 10	Taking Responsibility for Your Emotions	64
Chapter 11	The Courage to Be Vulnerable	69
Chapter 12	Risking Vulnerability ... Wisely	76
Chapter 13	When Vulnerability Hurts	82

PART THREE:
PURSUE PLEASURE, CHOOSE LOVE

Chapter 14	Permission to Feel Pleasure	93
Chapter 15	The Possibility of Pleasure	97
Chapter 16	Pleasure and Gratitude	100
Chapter 17	Your Pleasure Treasure Chest	101
Chapter 18	Give & Receive Love	106
Chapter 19	Control and Release	112
Chapter 20	Set Your Expectations	116
Chapter 21	Commit to the Practice	120
Chapter 22	Learn to Speak Love Languages	123
Chapter 23	When Your Needs Are Not Met	128
Chapter 24	When a Loved One Cannot Meet Your Needs	133

Conclusion 137

Self-Growth Exercises 141

   Part One Exercises: Practice Presence & Build Acceptance 142

      1. Checking in Tool 142

 2. Breaking the Trigger Pattern 143
 3. Somatic Practice of Connecting
   Love to Fear 143
 4. Write Your List 143
 5. Practice Holding Space with Children 144
 6. Remembering Your Choices 145
 7. Thich Nhat Hanh's "No earache today!" 145
 8. Red Flags 146

Part Two Exercises: Expand Compassion & Trust . . . 146
 1. Presence with Pain 146
 2. Shoring Up Inner Strength and Wisdom . . . 147

Part Three Exercises: Pursue Pleasure,
Choose Love. 147
 1. Pleasure-Seeking Practice 147
 2. Investigate your Relationship
   with Pleasure 148
 3. Gratitude Practice. 148
 4. Pleasure Treasure Chest Practice 149
 5. Self Love Meditation. 149
 6. Somatic Self-Massage Practice. 149
 7. Recognizing Physical Evidence of Love 150
 8. Release from Judgment —
   Internally and Externally. 151
 9. Change the Stories 151
 10. Love Languages Quiz 152
 11. Self-Inquiry Process with Desires 153

About the Author. 155

INTRODUCTION

What would it mean to you to know, deep in your bones, that you are finally capable of having healthy intimate partnerships?

What would it mean to you to feel so full of self-love that the notion of diving into dating again fills you with joy, delight, and excitement rather than dread and fear?

How would it be to trust that you will always feel safe, loved, and appreciated for the rest of your life no matter what hardships life throws your way?

How would your life change if you could know without question that you can have the most incredibly rich relationships with your family — relationships that are filled with trust, compassion, understanding, connection, and appreciation?

Would you like to learn how to expand your capacity for and experience of pleasure and joy exponentially?

Can you imagine what it would be like to feel 100% free and confident in giving and receiving support and love in all your relationships?

You can have all of this.

This book is your step-by-step guide for creating conscious relationships in all areas of your life by first building an authentic, bone-deep foundation of self-acceptance, self-trust, and self-love. This book is your guide for getting out of relationship ruts.

You have been working for years to change unhealthy relationship patterns. You understand the *why* behind them

— all your childhood baggage and traumas that created those familiar grooves in your brain — but you have not been able to find the *how* to change them. Instead, with every relationship, you find yourself digging deeper into those familiar ruts, like a car spinning its wheels in the mud, trying to get on a new path but only sinking deeper into the muck.

This book gives you the tools to fill in those ruts so that you can get out of the stuck place and create new paths forward in your relationships and your life. You begin by building up and strengthening your relationship with yourself because that is your foundation, the bedrock of your life. You then take the same steps to improve, strengthen, and deepen your relationships with everyone in your life — your partner, family, children, and close friends. Everything you learn about how to authentically love, honor, and trust yourself will be carried forward into building healthy, joyful, sustainable relationships in all areas of your life.

You picked up this book because you are struggling with relationships and with believing that real intimacy is possible. Most likely you've been struggling for a long time and have maybe even contemplated giving up and becoming a Buddhist monk, living a life free of attachments and intimate relationships.

At least, that's where I found myself several years ago.

After months of couples' therapy, I walked out of our therapist's office finally accepting the devastating truth that my marriage was over. For years I had been doing everything possible to blind myself from the reality that all that was left in my relationship with my ex-husband was resentment, hurt, anger, and disappointment. The strongest feeling in that moment was anger at him for all the ways I felt he had failed as a husband and a father. After a few weeks of seething with rage in survival mode — *Ask another mom to help with after-school pickups. Pack lunches the night before to get to work on time. Can I hire someone to shovel the driveway??* — I came

INTRODUCTION

to realize that all that anger was covering up other more debilitating emotions. I remember one moment so clearly in which I was sitting in my car, a few minutes early to pick up my daughter from preschool. I took the time to listen to my voicemail messages. There was one from an acquaintance, a woman I knew a bit from our kids going to school together, saying she had heard about my separation and wanted to check in on me; she was there if I needed to talk. This message knocked down the wall I had up around my feelings; I burst into uncontrollable, snotty, chest-shaking sobs. I was scared, sad, lonely, and overwhelmed, and more than anything I felt deeply ashamed of my failures. I realized then that I didn't think I deserved her sympathy and compassionate ear.

Over time, and with the help of an insightful and supportive therapist, I came to see that the ending of my marriage was not a simple black-and-white situation and it was ok for me to have a mix of feelings about it. My ex-husband had certainly failed in ways, and my anger at him was justified. I also needed to take responsibility for some of the failures in the relationship in order to grow and heal. Opening my eyes to that truth allowed me to understand the negative patterns that I had been perpetuating in intimate relationships and where they originated from in my childhood.

Through many hours on my therapist's couch I understood *why* I kept choosing men with substance abuse and/or mental health issues. I understood *why* I repeatedly put myself in the role of the martyr-caretaker partner.

Unfortunately, all this clarity and understanding did not address the question of how to change the patterns or how to make different choices in relationships. I still did not know how to create healthy, joyful, intimate relationships. Knowing *why* actually made the situation feel much worse because I would judge myself critically for not "getting it," not being able to get out of the old, tired, muddy ruts.

The truth is that it wasn't my fault that I didn't "get it" — and *it's not your fault either.*

You can't just fix your negative relationship patterns by wanting or wishing; it would be like trying to fix a pothole in the road by throwing a pretty rug across it. It takes focused effort, practice, and time to change deeply ingrained conditioning whether it's eating and exercise habits or relationship patterns. It will not come from reading a book (no, not even this one) or taking the advice of one of the gorgeous social media stars touting self-love and looking as if they have achieved enlightenment. When I was starting out on my healing journey, after admitting my marriage was over, I tried to follow their well-meaning advice, but usually, instead of inspiring me, it only added another layer or self-judgment and criticism: *Wow, Margot! You must be the only person in America that can't figure out this self-love stuff. What the hell is wrong with you? You are clearly just a broken person. Too messed up to fix.* My brain slid right into a downward spiral of victimhood, defeat, and self-recrimination, and I would pick up a bag of potato chips and watch *Hoarders* to make myself feel a little bit less like a loser.

Some part of me knew that there had to be helpful answers out there somewhere. I wasn't willing to give up and resign myself to suffering through unhealthy relationships for the rest of my life. I spent the next five years studying, learning, thinking about, and digging deeper and deeper into the question, "How can I have healthier, more joyful, more love-filled relationships?" I read dozens of relationship books and studied with the incredible Layla Martin and became a certified Sex, Love, and Relationship Coach. I coached and learned from hundreds of people about their heartbreak and relationships through my private coaching practice and Facebook groups.

And now, just six years later, I honestly feel like I'm living a miracle every day.

INTRODUCTION

Is the miracle that I am experiencing a healthy, joyful, romantic relationship with an amazing, emotionally mature man? In part. Even more miraculous, however, is that I have escaped the muddy rut of old familiar patterns. I have created new neural pathways in my brain and my path forward in my relationships is solid and clear to me. I know, without one shred of doubt, that I am worthy, deserving, and capable of incredibly healthy love no matter what happens with this particular man. I can say with complete honesty now that I love, honor, and trust myself always.

And the cherry on top is that I have filled my relationships with my children with more love, communication, and understanding. I have strengthened my relationships with my parents and sister, finding a path forward to more ease, joy, and compassion. I have come to a level of peace and positivity with my ex-husband. I have even brought my relationship with food to a healthier place than ever before! I feel grateful every day for the miracle that my life has become. I know that you can experience this miracle for yourself, and I can't wait any longer to show you how. Let's go.

PART ONE

Practice Presence & Build Acceptance

1
PRACTICE PRESENCE WITH YOURSELF

The first step out of your well-worn, unhealthy patterns and into healthy, joyful, supportive relationships with everyone in your life is to heal your relationship with yourself and build a rock-solid internal foundation of acceptance, trust, and love. *Why, you may ask, must I start here when it's my relationships with other people that need fixing?* You may be thinking, *I'm getting by okay most days.* Or, as an astute, somewhat skeptical client of mine recently put it, *What's the upside of creating more self-love?*

The answer is that the negative patterns that you see in your relationships with other people are all a reflection of negative patterns that you are stuck in with your relationship with yourself. Do you have abandonment issues with lovers? Do you find yourself with a hair-trigger temper with your children? Do you regularly feel unappreciated and misunderstood by your family? All of these situations result from your lack of acceptance, trust, and love for yourself: for *all* of yourself. The more you learn to acknowledge, accept, and love all the different parts of yourself, the more you will be able to acknowledge, accept, and love all the different parts of your loved ones.

Another reason to heal your relationship with yourself first is that it's good practice. If you've never had a relationship in which you felt seen, heard, and appreciated fully — whether with a friend, romantic partner, or even yourself — how will you know how to recognize it, much less receive it, when you meet someone who is willing and able to do that for you? Simply put: you won't. I know, I know, you're sure you would. You've been dreaming of such a relationship for years, after all. But trust me on this: I've seen it over and over again not only in my clients but also in myself. If you are used to being in relationships with narcissistic men, for instance, and then you meet a man who is thoughtful, empathetic, kind, and an amazing listener, your nervous system will short-circuit like a wet robot: "Does not compute! Error! Error!" will flash in big red letters inside your head. You will most likely either not feel attracted to this thoughtful man or do something subconsciously to push him away from you.

So, the first step is to do the inner work and practice on yourself. Learn how to listen, see, and appreciate all the different parts and subpersonalities of yourself first. Practice empathy and compassion with yourself. That way, when other people treat you properly, you will feel more familiar and comfortable and your nervous system will more easily accept it. Here's how a former client of mine Sarah, describes her journey toward greater self-acceptance.

I can always count on my ex-husband, Eddie, to trigger feelings of frustration and anger. I get infuriated when he forgets to bring Jack's soccer ball to practice or Sabrina's piano books to her lesson. However, when I remember to step back and examine my anger in these moments, something interesting happens: I realize that I also forget my kids' stuff regularly. What happens when I forget something for one of my kids? I get angry and frustrated with myself. I feel like a failure as a mom. When I can, I remind myself that I am doing the best I can and that it's impossible to be perfect in these situations.

And then I ask myself, "What if both Eddie and I are doing the best we can?"

I spent years trying to change my ex-husband's behaviors. I tried as many ways as I could think of to get him to remember things better. It never worked. He has changed himself over the years because he was ready to change and did his own work to accomplish it. That's always how it is. And now Eddie and I have an easy, pleasant, working relationship. Would this be the case if I had let my frustrations fill our relationship with anger? Definitely not. When I learned to accept the forgetful parts of myself, it not only built my self-acceptance and self-love, it allowed me to more easily accept similar parts in him.

GET TO KNOW YOURSELF

Now that we have covered the *why* of beginning your path towards healthy relationships by fixing your relationship with yourself, it's time to dive into the *how*.

Everywhere you look in our culture these days, there are messages telling you to love yourself more. But those well-meaning Instagram gurus and tampon commercials rarely tell you how to actually accomplish this feat. I want you to approach the goal of learning to love yourself with the same attitude that you would use when you begin to love another person — a new friend for instance. You may have felt an instant connection with this friend, but it took time to get to know them before you could feel deep trust, acceptance, and love, right? I want you to commit to just getting to know yourself first before even thinking about love. Makes sense, right?

Learn to Listen to Yourself

You get to know yourself better by practicing presence with all parts of yourself. You practice mindfulness with everything happening internally. In the simplest terms, mindfulness means that you pay close attention to everything that you feel — physically, emotionally and mentally — throughout your day. You may have done something similar if, for instance, you have ever tried to lose weight by practicing mindful eating or if you have practiced mindful breathing during meditation or yoga. In this case, I want you to be mindful in particular of your feelings, emotions, and messages from different parts of your body, checking in with yourself as often as possible.

Each of us has parts of ourselves that we are more comfortable listening to and allowing to be in charge of how we react and respond to other people and situations. Some people call this being a left- or right-brain thinker or say that a particular person leads with their heart rather than their head. I'm not too worried about what you call it so much as that you learn something about how to relate to yourself. The goal is to gather information, getting to know yourself without judgment or labels.

Checking in with Yourself

There is a great tool I call "checking in" that will help you begin to learn how to hear all the parts of yourself. I came up with it to help my clients who are first dipping their toes back into the dating pool after divorce, but you can use it at any time and in any situation. Checking in helps you navigate through the various confusing messages you may be hearing from different parts of your body in order to build internal connection and trust.

The first step is to identify your own goals and imagining how you will pursue them in a given scenario. You ask yourself two questions: *How do I want to feel in this upcoming situation?* And: *What am I trying to achieve?*

I taught this to a male client named Eric recently as he prepared for a first date. He had been chatting over the previous few months with a woman who was the manager at his local grocery store. He felt that she was interested in him, so he asked her out for dinner. When I spoke to him about his goals for the upcoming date he expressed his desire that she feel comfortable with him, that she have fun and laugh, and that he learn more about her. It's very common on a first date to think so much about the other person and forget to check in with yourself: Is she having a good time? Does she like me? Does she find me attractive? So, in our coaching session I asked him, "How do you want to feel on this first date?"

He took a few moments to think about it. "I want to feel confident, at ease, and like I'm being myself."

So, I asked him, "Can you remember a recent time in your life when you felt confident and at ease being yourself?"

"Yes," he replied, "When I was playing music at a gig." (He is not a professional musician but loves playing out with bands.)

"Perfect," I said, "Please close your eyes now. Allow yourself to bring up that memory. Really let your awareness be back in that moment of feeling so confident and at ease with yourself. What do you see and hear? What sensations do you feel in your body?

After a minute or so he said, "I feel warmth in my chest. It feels spacious and open. I feel like I'm standing in the 'Superman' pose, you know: feet wide, fists on hips. And I can feel the warmth flowing out of my chest into my arms. I feel my face relaxed and smiling."

"Wonderful" I said. "Let yourself just stay with that feeling for a few minutes. Really allow your nervous system to become comfortable and familiar with those sensations. Now stay present with this set of sensations and picture yourself about to meet Maria for your date. You are sitting at the bar, waiting for her to walk in the door. You turn and see her walking towards you. As you look at her, bring your awareness back to your body. Are there any new sensations present in this moment?"

"Yes," Eric says, "Now I feel nervous butterfly sensations in my stomach. I feel a constriction in my throat, and I've got tingling in my crotch now because she's gorgeous."

"Great," I say, "Now freeze the scene like you are pressing pause on a movie. Take a few deep breaths and let them out very slowly and steadily. Let yourself notice how you are spacious enough to be able to hold all these different sensations at the same time — you can feel both the 'Superman' feeling in your chest and the tightness in your throat, the butterflies in your belly and tingling in your pelvis. Recognize that you are the one observing, witnessing all these various sensations. And you are also thinking thoughts and listening to me and feeling your backside on the chair."

I gave him a few minutes to integrate that experience in silence before we discussed it.

What does an exercise like this accomplish? First, imagining beforehand the confusing mix of emotions and sensations that he will feel on his upcoming date allows him to practice "checking in" with himself while in a safe, supportive environment before trying it in the "real world." Secondly, getting the feel of his various emotions ahead of time lessens Eric's fear of them. Thirdly, realizing that nervousness, or any emotion for that matter, is not the only sensation present in a moment allows him to avoid getting overwhelmed by that emotion. He will be able to stay more present, centered, and calm.

Fourth, using this tool in a coaching session helped Eric clarify his specific goal for the evening. This in itself is enormously helpful. Going into any meaningful experience, whether it's a first date or a challenging conversation with your son, with a clear idea of what your authentic desires and goals are is a game-changer in relationships. Why? Let's look at Eric's goal again for his first date: to feel confident, at ease with himself, to get to know Maria better, and to make her feel comfortable.

Having this goal set for himself before the date begins helps him stay focused on paying attention to both how he feels and what signals she is sending him. Having a goal helps combat the nervousness and uncertainty that comes with any new situation in which you are allowing yourself to be vulnerable with another person. The questions that tend to spin around and around in anyone's head on a first date — *Does she like me? Is he attracted to me?* - get a little quieter because you can consciously bring your focus back to the goal.

Checking in with his own sensations also reminds Eric that although he can do his best to make his date feel comfortable and happy, she is also her own person with her own set of feelings, nerves, and hopes for the date. By recognizing his own confusing mix of sensations and thoughts, he is able to stay open with his date and not take it personally when she experiences and reacts to her own set of mixed sensations and thoughts.

For instance, imagine now that Eric and Maria are on their date, drinking some wine with dinner. The conversation is flowing and they both are enjoying themselves and feeling pretty comfortable. Imagine that at some point Eric is telling Maria a story about his job and he notices that her attention is starting to drift. She is looking away, fiddling with her fork and shifting in her seat.

In previous situations like this Eric would have immediately felt nervous. His mind would have started racing with judgmental thoughts such as, *Am I boring her? I'm talking too much!* or *This is a failure. She is not right for me. She is so rude; she's not even listening to my story.* The nervousness and critical thoughts would cause Eric to talk more, babbling without paying attention to the words coming out of his mouth, as his mind scrambled on how to "fix" the situation.

Having practiced the checking-in tool, however, Eric is able to pause in that moment and change this pattern. He brings his awareness back to the sensations inside himself, notices his racing mind, the tension in his throat, and the jitteriness in his legs. He takes a few deep breaths, stops talking, and asks Maria if she is okay.

She looks back at him, surprised, and says, "Yes. What you were saying just reminded me of something I forgot to do at work today. But I don't want to think about work right now — I would much rather be here with you than focused on work!"

What she probably did not say, but what she meant by her words and tone, was something like, "My mind started wandering. Thank you for noticing and bringing me back to the present." Because Eric stayed present to both himself and his date, he was able to help her also stay present.

Eric can check in with himself over and over and notice what he is feeling. The checking-in tool is meant to be used often and in all types of situations. Recalling a memory in which you felt the way you desire to feel all the time is very powerful. For Eric this was feeling confident and at ease in himself, as he does when playing music. This recall does two things. One, by holding that memory, Eric is actually retraining his nervous system to feel more comfortable when he feels confident and at ease. Neurologically, it's a similar process to learning a new physical skill: the more time he spends feeling confident and at ease, the easier it becomes to feel that way. Two, identifying the target feeling also helps him notice and identify red flags in the new situation. When he recognizes he is losing that feeling, he can figure out what is causing it and take action to remedy the situation immediately.

Advanced Check-In Tips

I recommend trying out this tool in your own life a few times this week, in various situations, as an experiment. Notice how it feels to use it. Notice how other people react to you when you are using it. You will eventually learn to become comfortable listening to the signals from all the parts of yourself.

It's no coincidence that our language assigns intelligence to various body parts. Recognizing that you sometimes "listen to your gut" or that you have a hard time "following your heart" or that you sometimes feel like your "penis has a mind of its own" is an incredibly helpful step in building a healthier relationship with yourself. You want to be able to consciously check in with parts of yourself to see how they are feeling and whether they have any wisdom to share about a particular situation. When you do this on a regular basis, you will be making decisions from a centered, grounded place. You will be building your confidence and trust in yourself on your own healing path and helping you handle the many kinds of difficulties that can arise in relationships with loved ones.

Pay particular attention to when it is easy for you to remember to check in with yourself and what situations you look back on and wish you had checked in. Remember: this is a new muscle you are building. It's called a practice because it is not a skill you can master perfectly right out of the box. Every person has parts of themselves that they shy away from, and in situations that trigger those parts it will be much harder to stay mindful. It is one thing to learn to listen to the parts of you that feel good, confident, joyful, light, at ease, and proud, but it takes even more focus and courage to listen to the parts of you that cause painful feelings such as shame, fear, sadness, or regret.

In my experience, a clear majority of both men and women have a difficult time allowing themselves to feel and show sadness. There can be a deep fear of allowing oneself to feel sadness because it can cause you to feel weak, vulnerable, and overwhelmed. In addition, it can be difficult to allow yourself to feel sad as an adult if you grew up in a household in which the adults did not know how to handle their children's sadness.

As a parent I know how triggered I get when I see one of my children feeling sad. My instinct to "fix the problem" is immediate and powerful. *What have I done wrong? I'm a terrible mother! He will hate me forever if I don't make him feel better.* This is an uncomfortable, frightening, debilitating way to feel.

For many people, myself included, anger is often a more comfortable emotion to feel then sadness. It feels less vulnerable and therefore safer. A wise person once said, "Anger is the bodyguard of sadness." Indeed, anger is often a part of you that developed early in life to protect you from suffering and feeling scared. Those protector parts are very sensitive and work hard to keep you safe. The especially difficult part is that these protector pieces of your psyche developed when you were a small child and therefore may trigger you to respond like a small child well into adulthood. The ever-alert protectors get reinforced and stronger every time you experience an intense trauma. They can cause you to react as if the intense trauma is occurring in the present, whenever you get triggered, when often what is happening in that moment is not a real threat.

Declare a Truce with the Protectors

How do you begin to change your relationship to these difficult emotions that your protector parts, vigilantly working to shield you from pain, have buried deep inside you? How do you learn to acknowledge and just accept that they are part of you?

First, you have to figure out which emotions trigger the strongest reaction in you. You may already have an idea about some of them. Others may be buried too deeply under layers of protection for you to notice immediately. A good place to begin is to look at what triggers anger often in your closest relationships. Remember that the areas that your protector parts work hardest to shield are those that formed in your earliest years and/or in response to the most intense trauma.

For example, like many of us, I get triggered very strongly when I feel rejected by a loved one. Who hasn't felt rejected by someone they love at some point in their childhood? In my case, the deep wounding resulted from a childhood situation with my sister in which she suddenly, and without explanation, shut herself off from any relationship with me. (I learned as an adult that she had been suffering from debilitating clinical depression, but I had no knowledge of that as a child. I felt just like Anna in the film *Frozen* with her sister and best friend suddenly acting like a completely different person and rejecting me completely.)

Not surprisingly, in my adult life, the experience of a loved one being "with me" one minute and then "gone" the next can trigger a powerful emotional response. Perhaps we were texting quickly back and forth and then all of a sudden he stops writing back to me. In those moments I would react in one of two ways. I would either feel incredible anxiety and panic: racing heart, shaky legs, shallow breathing. Or I would feel intensely angry and lash out at him through aggressive, angry texts. The panic and anxiety was the result of my psyche feeling as if it was back in the original trauma situation; the excessive anger was my tough, vigilant protectors working to block any perceived threat of pain.

Does any of the above sound familiar to you? I'd be surprised if you couldn't recall a time even in the past few days when you reacted with panic or extreme anger to a situation that you later realized was quite benign. We all do it (except maybe the Dalai Lama.)

What can you do about it? The first step is always the same: *learn as much as you can about yourself* in all your complexity. What situations cause the protectors to show up? How do your protectors tend to handle things? Do they encourage you to get loud and angry? Maybe punch that jerk in the face? Do they encourage you to remove yourself from the situation either by physically fleeing or emotionally shutting down? Some people actually fall asleep when triggered into a fear state. Or do your protectors encourage you to numb yourself in some way? Have another shot of whiskey. Eat that entire tub of ice cream.

When you can recognize the moments that you are in a triggered state, you can learn to change your reaction and actions. First, stop whatever you are doing or saying. Take a breath and start counting in your head. Focus on counting and breathing. Count until you feel yourself come back to calmness. Then begin to focus your awareness on the physical sensations present in your body. Notice the thoughts that are present in your mind. Do nothing else, say nothing else, until you feel calm and centered again.

I share an amazing tool in the Self Development Exercises section of this book called *Somatic Practice of Connecting Fear and Love* that will help you come back to a feeling of safety and peace after getting triggered. This is a tool you will first practice at home and then eventually feel comfortable enough to use in the "real world" when interacting with other people.

Each of us carries patterning in our bodies and brains that developed during our childhood and teenage years. Unfortunately for all humans, the negative and painful experiences tend to get imprinted more intractably than the positive moments. Our brains and bodies remember and hold onto trauma, hurt, rejection, shame, and fear and then develop defensive strategies to try to protect ourselves from those painful feelings. [1]

The defensive strategies that you developed when you were young have been working hard to protect you from pain throughout your life. It is especially crucial for you to practice patience and non-judgment when getting to know

---

[1] If you want to explore more about the neuroscience of trauma, I suggest reading *The Body Keeps The Score* by Bessel van der Kolk, a tough but fascinating read.

these protector parts of yourself. They are akin to mother bears protecting their babies from hunters — fierce and strong. When they sense danger they will often cause you to act in ways that you are uncomfortable with. For some people this can manifest as anger and an aggressive temper, for others it can be freezing emotionally and stonewalling or physically fleeing a situation. Another common defensive strategy is the adoption of a "snarky teenager" attitude: *This is stupid. I don't need this. I'm better than this.*

You may be accustomed to trying to fight against or simply ignore these defensive strategies when they arise in you. I am asking you to *stop doing that.* These protectors aren't something to fight against or try to banish from your body.

It is actually counterproductive to your goal of healthy relationships to try to ignore these parts or wish them away. First, because that battle takes a lot of energy and time and you most likely will not win it. These parts of you have years of practice fighting and will respond to aggression with aggression. In addition, if your goal is to love yourself more and feel better about yourself, then you have to accept and love all the parts of yourself — including the parts that make you uncomfortable. Remember that the world and all of us creatures in it have light and dark, growth and decay, beauty and ugliness. If you want to fully accept and love yourself, then you have to accept and love all of yourself, especially the parts you tend to shy away from because of fear, sadness, or anger. These parts most need your acceptance and compassion if you are to have a happy, peaceful life with healthy, joyful relationships.

Declare a truce within yourself — literally. You can even give it a time limit if that feels reassuring. Something like: *I declare a truce of one month in the war I have been waging against myself.*

When you put down the sword you've been wielding against yourself for so many years in the form of self-judgment and criticism, you will experience the most incredibly delicious level of freedom in your life. And laying down your sword, perhaps surprisingly, actually increases your ability to change parts of yourself that you wish to change. For now, the important practice is to just accept all the parts of yourself that show up as you check in and practice mindfulness.

Another incredibly helpful result of laying down your self-judgment sword is that it allows you to dig deeper with honesty and acceptance into what is most important to you in your close relationships. Do you know what you want in your relationships? Have you ever taken the time to ask yourself that? How do you want to feel in your relationship with your children? With your parents? With your boyfriend, girlfriend, husband, or wife?

By the way, don't worry if you have never asked yourself these questions: you are in the right place to ask them now.

You have to decide what brings you the most joy, peace, and delight in all of your relationships, and this may look different for every person and every relationship you are in.

Just as every person has to decide what to eat to make themselves feel their best, every person has to make their relationship choices that will feel the healthiest and most delightful. You may consider yourself a very healthy eater but still acknowledge that not all healthy food is delicious. You may love avocados but hate brown rice. You may go gaga for broccoli but despise kale. Your idea of a healthy relationship may be seeing your partner on Saturday nights, while someone else might need more time with their romantic interest. Your ideal relationship with your mother might be a daily phone call, while others find a once-a-year visit to be desirable.

Although everyone's food and relationship choices will be individual, there are some commonalities that I have observed though my personal and professional circles. Everyone wants to feel heard and seen by the person they are in relationship with. They want to be appreciated for who they authentically are, to be acknowledged for things they do for people they care about. They want to trust the people they are in close relationships with — trust that they are not lying or misleading them, and that they are honest about who they are and how they feel about them. They want to be forgiven when they mess up. They want to feel that they make the other person happy and feel good.

Most people also want relationships to feel fun and easy. They want to feel pleasure when with the other person — no matter what they are doing — more often than pain and struggle. They want to feel a close bond between themselves and the other person and to share mutual respect. They want to have faith and trust in their love for one another.

I am talking about not just romantic relationships but all kinds of relationships. I believe that almost everything can be healed and made joyful, free, and effortless when looked at through the lens of relationships. The above applies for romantic relationships as well as your relationships with your children, your friends, and your family. There is a fun, easy exercise in the Self-Growth Exercises section called *Write Your List* that can help you dive into this inquiry into how you define healthy, joyful relationships for yourself.

FACING DOWN RESISTANCE

It is crucial at this point to discuss another universal but often overlooked situation that you may notice as you check in with yourself. You may be experiencing it right now, as you read these words. It may be manifesting as an internal voice saying, *You don't need to read this book.* Or, *Hmm, I wonder if there's any chocolate cake leftover from yesterday?* Or it may manifest as a sudden sleepiness and desire to nap. These reactions fall into the category of "resistance."

I use the word resistance for any and all feelings and thoughts that arise in you that try to block you from taking action towards a healthier, happier you. Resistance takes many forms and occurs at different times for different people and in different situations. Resistance almost always shows up when you grow and move closer to your truth. That resistance comes from your internal armor, those same protectors that have been trying to keep you safe all these years. The protectors snap to attention here because change and growth feel threatening and scary to your nervous system. If you did not feel resistance, you probably would not need to do this work.

So how do you handle this resistance? The first step is to recognize resistance for what it is and what role it plays in your life. Again, it is not something to hate or try to banish from your body. You can just notice it — even greet it like a familiar if rather annoying acquaintance. Just this act alone of acknowledging the resistance without judgment or aggression shifts your relationship with it and creates more space for connection and trust.

To be clear, feeling resistance to growing, learning, and changing is different from the feelings and thoughts that try to prevent you from doing something that is not in your best interest. For example, I feel resistance almost every time I sit down at my computer to write. My brain starts telling me: *You need to put some laundry in. Go check Facebook. You should definitely pluck your eyebrows. Oh my God! The plants need watering!*

It can be difficult sometimes to decipher between feelings of resistance and a clear internal "no," but with practice, you become more and more familiar with your own signals. Usually a clear "no" actually feels quite good in your body; it has less of a charge around it. For instance, every year, at my daughter's school they do an overnight sleepover where the kids and parents set up tents outside and everyone camps out. This sounds to me like the third level of hell. The only thing that would make sleeping on the hard, cold ground without running water worth it for me would be if I were in some extraordinary spot in nature enjoying the quiet peacefulness of being away from civilization. But sleeping on the cold, hard ground, surrounded by screechy children hopped up on s'mores and knowing they have the chance to stay up late with their friends? That is a clear "no freaking way" for me. When I say no to doing the campout with my kids, I feel pleasant sensations of calm and peace in my body. I also feel a little bit of mom guilt, but I recognize that this is a different feeling than internal resistance.

2

PRACTICE PRESENCE WITH OTHERS

Now that you have been practicing presence with all the parts of yourself, you can bring this same practice into all of your close personal relationships. Learning how to be present for all your loved ones is unquestionably one of the most important skills to master in order to create healthy, joyful, sustainable relationships. Being present with another person means that you see them, hear them, and accept them exactly as they are. Your ego, feelings, and desires recede to create more space for the other person in the interaction.

The Need to Be Seen

Why is being present so important? Think about a close relationship in your life that feels healthy, joyful and easy. Answer the question, "Why do I enjoy spending time with this person so much?" I would be willing to bet a million dollars that what came up for you was some variation of, "I feel heard and seen by him/her. I feel appreciated for who I am. I feel loved by them. We get each other."

Whatever else one may desire in relationships, the need to be seen, heard, and appreciated is basic and universal.

PRACTICE PRESENCE WITH OTHERS

This is true for men, women, colleagues, children, romantic partners, friends, family, old, and young; it's true for Americans, Brazilians, Italians, Indians, and so on. There are endless subtle and not so subtle variations within human experience, but the need to be seen, appreciated, and loved for who we are is one of the beautiful, pervading themes of human life.

You learn to hold space for another person by first learning to be present for yourself. In the first section you practiced presence with all the parts of yourself. You began to acknowledge and accept your resistance, challenging emotions, and other protector parts. You laid down the sword you have been wielding against yourself and declared a truce from all negative, self-judging thoughts in order to create space for more self-acceptance and trust. This is where you start to see how to apply these new skills in relationship to other people.

Imagine your best friend, Peter, excitedly shares with you about a new job offer. It's everything he wanted: good pay, good company, great benefits. "I'm so relieved and excited, but I'm also pretty nervous," he tells you. You respond, "Why are you nervous?! This is what you've always wanted!" Peter sort of shrugs and says, "Yeah, I know, I know, I'm not complaining," and then he changes the subject.

Can you see how this was a missed opportunity for connection? In this instance, you react in response to past experiences with your friend instead of being present to what he is feeling and experiencing in the moment. It's not that what you said is untrue — it's just not pertinent right then. Peter would feel so much more support from you if you said something like, "I hear you. It sounds like an exciting opportunity, but I get why you would be nervous about it, too."

Let's push the illustration further. What if, as Peter continues talking about his new job, you start thinking, *How come he gets to move ahead while I'm stuck in this dead end position?* Or, *I bet he'll get to travel, see the world, making new friends. He won't have time for me anymore.* Jealousy, anger, and resentment are all normal, common reactions. I'm not asking you to stifle these feelings or be ashamed or critical of yourself for having them. Although you cannot control your emotions, you can learn to recognize, understand, and control your response and reaction to them. When you try to pretend feelings don't exist or shame yourself about them, you will not be able to control how you handle them. Sometimes all you need to do is take a deep breath and center yourself in the present moment.

Then, after congratulating Peter and acknowledging his nervousness, you might say, "Good for you, Peter. I'm happy for you. Honestly, I'm a little jealous, too." This honest sharing may open up the opportunity for further connection with Peter and a discussion about your job situation.

Holding Space

When you are staying present to another's emotions while also acknowledging your own, we call this "holding space." Holding space for someone else can also lead to gaining clarity for yourself. In the situation with Peter, you may become conscious, possibly for the first time, of your dissatisfaction with your job, by noticing your reactions to his news. Now Peter gets the opportunity to hold space for you. If he feels supported, he might say, "Really? Jealous? I thought you loved your job!" This can lead to you gaining more clarity on your work situation, and give more opportunities for building trust and understanding between the two of you. Win-win!

Being present, like many of the other skills needed to build healthy, joyful, sustainable relationships, does not come easily. It takes practice. I still have not mastered it myself. If anything, I have had to master the ability to apologize, after the fact, when I missed an opportunity to be present for a friend, romantic partner, or family member.

It is crucial to work on this skill because it is what we ourselves most desire from the people we have close relationships with. When you hold space for people in your life, you create possibilities for honest communication and authentic connection. This is how you build an honest, real foundation in every relationship.

When you fail to practice presence in a close relationship, you fail to fully understand the other person. This usually leads to resentment, frustration, hurt, and anger. This is true in all relationships, even though it will manifest differently for each type and take slightly different skills to master. Next we will go deeper into how to practice presence in specific types of relationships.

3

PRESENCE WITH YOUR CHILDREN

If you are not a parent, feel free to jump ahead to the next section on presence with your family. For you parents out there, I believe this section contains transformative advice on how to improve your relationships with your kids.

People regularly tell me, "You have incredible kids," and, "Your kids are so well-behaved.' My cousin Dan told me, "I want to have kids because your kids are so awesome!" Waiters and waitresses regularly compliment me on their behavior, and I love parent-teacher conferences because I always receive glowing reports. And even though my son and daughter are very different from each other, this is true for both of them.

I am not trying to boast, here. The last thing I want is to come off as a know-it-all perfect parent casually dispensing advice to others as if I have it all figured out. I've followed those people's blogs and Instagram feeds and know how much shame and doubt you can heap on yourself when your life isn't as easy and neat as theirs.[2] The truth is I have spent a good amount

---

[2] When my infant son had trouble sleeping for longer than an hour straight, I read a million books that promised me a solution. The little smidgeon of confidence I had as a mom swooshed down the drain as

of time trying to understand what role I might be having in my children's behavior. In fact, I originally thought people were just being nice until I learned that not all my friends had this experience. Then I sought a deeper understanding of what was going on..

To begin with, each and every child is unique and needs different things from the adults in his or her life. This, as much as anything, is why parenting advice can appear to conflict or just not work. But there are certain universal needs that all humans have, adults and children alike, such as to be seen, heard, appreciated, and loved for who we truly are. I made my share of parenting mistakes, but I believe that by continually focusing on improving my ability to be present and hold space for my children, I have helped them to become the respectful, confident, joyful, and compassionate young people that they are.

Although we've spoken about the universal need to be present for others, we should acknowledge that being present for your children presents unique challenges. You are responsible for their physical and emotional needs; you are responsible for making them feel safe and loved; and you are responsible for preparing them to navigate the world and have healthy relationships with others. Your words and actions mold their impressionable young psyches, creating lifelong neural pathways. Your voice will be one of the loudest voices in their heads when they grow up. Will that voice be supportive, loving, and appreciative or accusing, demeaning, and condemning?

You are responsible for all of this while also remembering that their needs change as they develop; your relationship with them as well as your responsibilities towards them will change

---

expert after expert offered conflicting advice. I do not doubt that the authors meant well, but I was left feeling that the entire parenting book industry, unfortunately, often only heightens new moms' and dads' fears and insecurities.

as you scramble to keep up. No relationship is static, but this is triple true with your children. Life with kids is a constant dance between responding to the immediacy of their feelings, desires, hopes, fears, disappointments, frustrations — all the dailiness of their lives — and pulling back to see the bigger picture, their long-term needs. By *long-term needs* I mean their need to become their own person rather than the person you and/or society wants them to be. In other words, you have to see the forest as well as the trees. Being able to navigate my way through all of these challenges is the most difficult, rewarding, and sacred part of my life.

While your relationship with your child may be the most sacred, it is also likely to be the most challenging one you will ever have. Why? Because kids tend to act like ... well ... kids. They can be thoughtless and self-absorbed. They can also trigger the heck out of you. The intense love and sense of sacred responsibility you feel towards them makes you especially vulnerable to them. Added to this is the normal fear that your child's every action reflects on you.[3] And of course, there is the additional pressure that comes from knowing that other people are constantly judging your parenting skills: everyone from strangers at the grocery store to your own parents.

This responsibility may seem overwhelming at first, but the good news is that children are, in general, quite understanding and forgiving. When I have a misunderstanding with one of my children, it literally takes less than five minutes to resolve it and move on. Can you say that about a misunderstanding with any adult in your life?

---

[3] For example, when my kid forgets her coat at school, I often feel angry and guilty: *I am not raising her to value her belongings. I am not raising her to think ahead. How is she going to survive as an adult if she can't remember her coat when it's 30 degrees outside?! Do the other parents think I sent her to school without a coat in December?*

Soccer Practice
A few weeks ago, I picked up my son, Oliver, from soccer practice. It was late, cold, and dark, and I had been shuttling around for what felt like hours — pick up from school, drive to sewing club, drive home, cook dinner, drop off at soccer, drive home, monitor piano, drive back. I was grumpy and hungry when my son came ambling off the field, chatting with his teammates, and got in the car excited to tell me how great he played in practice. My anger was triggered and I basically growled at him to hurry up and fasten his seat belt. That night when I was tucking him into bed, he said, "Mom I feel like sometimes you don't tell me you're proud of me very much."

I was horrified that he would feel that way. I took a moment to take a slow deep breath and asked him, Are you saying that because of how I snarled at you after practice?

He nodded.

I apologized for my behavior and explained how I had been tired and hungry and beginning to feel resentful about how much chauffeuring I do but how that was no excuse for rudeness. He accepted my apology, forgave me, and even thanked me for driving him to his many activities. We hugged, and that was that. Being aware and honest about what triggered my short temper with Oliver turned what could have been a long-remembered, resentful moment between us into one that instead solidified the love and trust within our relationship.

Holding Space for Your Kids: The Inner Work

I have found that there are two different ways that you need to really hold space for your kids, which correspond to inner work and outer work. The inner work involves bringing awareness to your own patterns and triggers with your kids, as in my soccer practice example. This step alone can radically shift your experience in a moment because it causes you to pause and self-examine. That pause creates the space you need to break out of an old pattern and respond in a different way.

To become aware of your patterns and triggers you again need to practice being present to your own emotions and reactions in a given moment. Begin to practice on your own using a memory of a recent experience with your child. Think back to a time in which you lost your temper or felt very angry or irritated with your child. There might also be regular moments within your daily routine that always seem to trigger you. Is it when your kid doesn't do their chores without you asking three times? Or when it seems to take them forever to get ready for school? Or maybe it happens when your kid is struggling to understand their math homework. Take a minute now to think or write down which activities, attitudes, or words from your kids most regularly trigger you to behave in a way that you later regret.

Now pick one example from your list, close your eyes, and put yourself back in that moment. Ask yourself, *What story did I hear in that moment?* In other words, *What did my child's behavior mean to me?* Take a few moments to write down what comes up. When you have done this a few times, notice what stories or thoughts are recurrent. You may notice, for example, that you have repeatedly heard a voice say, *Oliver doesn't respect me. He takes me for granted.* Or, *Isadora is so lazy — just like her dad!* Now ask yourself, *Do I know this to be true 100%?* Take the next few moments to think about and write down evidence that contradicts the above thoughts.[4]

One of the most valuable practices that I developed for holding space for my children is remembering and taking responsibility for the choices I made to bring me to that

---

[4] See Self-Growth Exercise #5 *Unpacking Triggers with Your Kids* for a more detailed explanation of this practice.

moment with them. In the above situation with my son, I admitted to him that I had been short-tempered because of being tired and hungry and starting to feel resentful. I wasn't blaming him though. I remember that I chose to have children. I choose to encourage them to pursue activities such as soccer and piano. I choose to cook healthy food for them when another choice on an evening like that could have been to order pizza. And in that moment, tired and hungry as I was, would I make a different choice on any of those questions? Definitely not. Coming back to that truth is incredibly helpful.

HOLDING SPACE FOR YOUR KIDS: THE OUTER WORK

The second way to hold space for your kids is to teach them how to practice presence with themselves. I find this helpful especially because kids usually have fewer choices than they would like in how to spend their time. We make them go to school, do homework, take showers, put the video games down, etc. But they still do have choices, in their lives, throughout their day, and it is empowering to guide their attention to those places. When you practice presence with your kids you learn that they can be great teachers themselves. Young children, in general, are very present with themselves (which ironically is one of the things that can be so triggering for grownups, say, when you want them to finish goofing around and get ready for bed!).

I recently had a proud mama moment watching my son teach his younger sister this lesson. She was complaining about something called "Reading Buddies" that she does at her school. It's a time once a week in which all the kids in her class read a book aloud to younger kids. She complained that the little kids didn't sit still and listen to her. My son, who had to do the same activity four years earlier, responded to her with, "Oh, yeah! That used to get on my nerves, too. But then I figured out a way to make it more fun." Izzy inquired skeptically about how he managed to do that. Oliver replied, "I just remembered that they are little kids that look up to me, just like you used to when you were four years old and I would read to you! I felt happy that I could be like a role model to little kids."

I developed another tool that has proven invaluable for myself, my kids, and my clients called "No earache today!" after hearing a Thich Nhat Hanh talk. He gently and non-judgmentally questions, "Why does nobody wake up every morning and celebrate: 'I do not have an earache right now! My toes do not hurt today!'?" The tool is that simple: practice feeling gratitude every morning during breakfast for a few little things. With practice, it becomes easier and easier to focus on the positive parts of your day.

It is human nature to focus on anything negative before anything positive: to wake up every morning and immediately focus on all the negatives, all your aches and pains. Similarly, it is easy to focus on the hard parts of raising kids and the parts of them that we wish we could change or even "fix." Truthfully though, you can be grateful for every day you have with your children in which they are alive, free, and healthy.

You can even begin to feel grateful for when they act grumpy or sassy. My daughter growls at me when I call her cute. Now as much as I wish I could call her cute all the time (because she is super freaking cute), I love that she resists being labeled that way. She sees herself as a fierce, part-ninja/part-cat artist. This view of herself leads her to sometimes argue with me and act very sassy. And without a doubt, I get annoyed. But when I can, I remember how grateful I am that her self-image is so strong, fierce, and fiery. I would not change that for anything.

4

PRESENCE WITH PARENTS AND SIBLINGS

Holding space and being present for your parents and other close family relatives is at least as tricky a proposition as attempting it with your kids, but for different reasons. There's just so much baggage with parents, right? The baggage comes from many sources, but it generally comes down to the fact that you wish they were different than they are. Indeed, you have pretty specific concepts of how you would like them to speak and act and so on. But while you can expect a certain level of respect from people, you cannot expect them to be everything you want them to be. Instead, when you can accept your parents and siblings for who they are *in the moment*, it gradually becomes easier to feel at peace and even filled with gratitude. This creates the space needed for your time together to feel much more comfortable and pleasant.

In my case, I suffered for years under the illusion that everything my parents did reflected somehow on who I was. I spent years feeling embarrassed by my parents because I perceived everything they did or said as an extension of my own personality or actions. For instance, my father used to have a very short and hot temper (before he mellowed with age!), and he has always had enormous difficulty with being kept waiting — *for anything*. When I was young, I would feel mortified when he would regularly bark and snap at hostesses and waitresses. I remember thinking, *This woman must think I'm a jerk too! She's going to hate me!* This is what psychologists call "enmeshment," the inability to separate your own feelings and experiences from others', and people who get in patterns of unhealthy relationships often struggle with it. I needed to learn clear boundaries and recognize that not only is my dad's behavior not reflective on me at all, but I can never control another person's feelings towards me in a given situation, anyway. There was no way for me to know what those women were thinking or feeling in the moment. Getting worked up about it was just a waste of time and energy on my part.

I also spent years feeling hurt and angry that neither of my parents ever told me they were proud of me. I remember the moment a few years ago when I gathered the courage to say this directly to my mom. Her initial response was defensive, "Well, you don't share with me about the work you do! I don't know enough about it to know whether to be proud of you or not!" At the time, I was the manager of a large-scale free meal program, feeding upwards of 400 at-risk people hot meals daily. Her response increased my anger and resentment because I didn't think she needed to know a whole lot more to at least feel *some* pride. I remained silent, however, taking deep breaths and practicing presence with myself. After a few moments, my mom said, in a different tone, "You know, I don't really know how to say I'm proud of you. It's just not something I ever learned from my parents or anyone else for that matter. It feels very uncomfortable for me." Hearing her honest, vulnerable response helped to diffuse the uncomfortable feelings inside my body. She was doing the best she could. I could acknowledge that I still felt some anger and resentment at the same time as understanding and compassion for her. From there, I remembered that I felt proud of *myself* for the work I was doing at the soup kitchen (as well as for many other accomplishments in my life) and that I could let go of my attachment to receiving that from my mother.

I'm not excusing either of my parents' behaviors, but taking their actions or lack of actions personally made it impossible for me to be clear and present for them. In turn, I was unable to appreciate them for who they actually are and all their wonderful qualities. My dad's lack of patience with delays, for instance, stems from his devotion to creating enjoyable experiences for his loved ones and a desire to insure our happiness. He recently spent many hours (and a ton of money) planning every detail of an incredible family adventure to Costa Rica. My mother, despite her discomfort in verbalizing that she is proud of me, has spent hours upon hours reading this very manuscript and editing the first draft! It seems the most helpful lesson that I have learned about how to have healthy, joyful relationships with my parents is to focus on letting go of the *shoulds* without judging myself for wishing things were different and to remind myself to not take their actions towards me or anyone else personally. I come back to the trust, respect, and love I have for myself in challenging moments, and when I am calm and centered, shift my focus to the positive impact they have on my children's' and my lives.

Practicing presence becomes even more important as your parents age and/or get sick. Just as our children constantly grow and change, so do aging parents. If you want to enjoy your time with them before they die, you can choose to let go of past baggage as much as possible and hold space for them as they are today.

Of course, you can choose not to do this as well. You may have had abusive or neglectful parents, so it may be a healthier choice for you to move on with your life, separate from them. It is always your choice.

I have learned the most about how to practice presence and to let go of wishing people were different than they are in my relationship with my sister. My sister and I used to be close as kids, but as we grew up we somehow grew apart. For years, I wanted so desperately for us to have a close, loving relationship again. I wanted to feel close to her, for her to be close to my kids. For a long time, I clung to the idea that there was something I could do or say, that if I worked hard enough on the relationship I could restore what was lost.

And then one day, after studying this concept of holding space and being present, I happened to be with my sister over Thanksgiving holiday. We were discussing, of all things, the Game of Thrones books. She was explaining to me how she had written out charts in order to keep track of the relationships between the hundreds of characters. I was astonished and amused. I had handled the torrent of characters by deciding to just ignore certain characters altogether. All of a sudden, I had a moment of incredible clarity, like clouds parting overhead and a ray of sunshine came down. In that instant I saw her clearly for maybe the first time in my life. I saw how fundamentally different we are, how our paths in this lifetime have led us and continue to lead us in very different directions. I realized that there is no magic action I could take or words I could say to transform our relationship.

The incredible part was that this realization actually led me to feel easier in my love for her, less disappointed by the lack of a meaningful connection with her in that moment. I realized she doesn't owe me anything. There is no unwritten law of the universe that says I get to have an amazingly close relationship with my sister. Just like there is no rule that says I get to be a great singer. As they say in my daughter's school: "You get what you get, and you don't get upset."

When you let go of feelings such as *it isn't right* or *it's unfair* that the person you care about is not behaving the way you wish they would and accept the undeniable reality of the situation, it feels like letting go of a huge breath you've been holding in. That exhalation creates space for more compassion, understanding, and love within that relationship.

Is it inevitable that you will be disappointed and let down sometimes by the people closest to you? Maybe not inevitable, but certainly very likely. The more that you can practice holding space and show up open-minded and open-hearted in each moment with your parents, children, and siblings, however, the better your chances are of appreciating them for who they are and thereby feeling less disappointment, hurt and resentment.

5

PRESENCE WITH ROMANTIC PARTNERS

Being present and holding space with lovers and romantic partners presents its own particular challenges because of how attached you get to them as well as how attached you get to all the stories you tell yourself about them. It is not easy to stay present with and really let yourself see and hear the truth of a person whom you are having a whirlwind of romantic, oxytocin-fueled feelings for. Holding space for intimate partners begins at the very beginning of relationships when you're only dating and continues throughout every long-term relationship.

In long-term relationships, it is so easy to fall into a certain groove with each other that you don't even notice it happening. You begin to think, *I know this person so well*, when in fact you may have ceased really being present for them in each moment. It's also incredibly easy for conscious presence to lapse in relationships because of misleading cultural narratives. Popular films, TV, and music all encourage you to think of love as something that happens to you rather than something you decide to engage with and focus on.

Have you ever been to the pet store on Adopt a Rescue day? Every time I walk in to that scene, my heart melts. Even now, writing about it, I feel the "Aw" waiting to come up and out of my throat. I feel the warm softness heating up in my chest and the voice in my head saying loud and clear, *Take each of those cuties home! It will be okay. They need you!* I fall in love with each and every dog I see the second it looks at me with its big eyes. Love at first sight, every time.

But is my house filled with adopted dogs? No, it isn't, because I recognize that despite the love I feel for each of them, it's not in my best interest — nor theirs — to make them all mine on that day.

It's not easy. Just like it is not easy to resist falling into a relationship with every person that makes you feel gooey and warm inside. I do not mean that you want to choose intimate relationships with a person that does not make you feel warm and gooey — that feeling is very important — but there is more to real intimacy. In fact, there is work to do. You start at warm and gooey and then begin the process of actually seeing, hearing, and understanding who that person is, on as many levels and as deeply as possible, before committing to being in relationship with them.

At this point you may be thinking, *I don't know how to get past warm and gooey. I don't even know what I need or want in a relationship! I always make the wrong choices for myself.* Chances are very good that if you picked up this book, you are someone who has a history of unhealthy, even dysfunctional relationships. Chances are also good that you have a certain awareness of your own patterns that you wish you could change and a pretty solid understanding of why and how they developed originally.

Mindfulness in relationships means developing an understanding of what you want in a healthy relationship. Many people spend more time thinking about what features and functions they want in their next car than on the habits and qualities of their next romantic partner. But practicing presence outside of relationships is crucial for learning about what you want and how to change your patterns and make different choices. You can begin to learn how to practice presence in your relationships with an exercise called Red Flags that teaches you to examine past relationships. In order to be able to learn how to begin to make different choices in your future, you have to spend energy and focus to learn from your past. This is where deep healing will occur.

To illustrate the Red Flags exercise, and how you can bring presence to a past relationship, I want to share a personal story about an ex-boyfriend whom I will call Joel. Taking time to do this exercise has allowed me to use some of my deepest pain into some of my most profound healing and growth.

Joel and I connected through a dating app and then met at a cozy little coffee shop for our first date on a blustery January afternoon. My initial impression was that he was way more attractive than his pictures — very handsome face: strong chin, high cheekbones, and piercing electric-blue eyes. He radiated an intense, coiled-up energy.

I remember sitting across from him, all bundled up from the cold but feeling extremely hot in my face, having "perma-grin," the whole time we talked. I remember feeling excited that a person who was so charismatic and had such intense energy inside him might be interested in me. There was a feeling of "being chosen" by him that made me feel special.

I did not "fall in love" on that first date. I remember having some reservations about him. I found some of his views on politics to be bordering on paranoid and not based in reality. I felt no tingling, turned-on sensations in my body when we kissed at the end of the date. Neither did I experience the warm, gooey feeling in my chest that is a sign of connection and trust for me.

I like to get a second impression of people, though, so we went out again. That time I did start to feel the warm, soft sensations in my chest. He was a sweet and compassionate person. We had so much fun together — hiking, exploring, and cooking together. When I looked at him I saw his inner strength, intelligence, integrity, and passion. I created stories in my mind of us traveling together, leading healing retreats, and having wild adventures together. I imagined us growing old together: holding hands and sitting quietly on a porch in some beautiful place, feeling that we had lived life to the fullest, loved as much and as openly as we could, raised amazing human beings, and reached our potential.

Beautiful story, right? In fact, it was not a story of true mindfulness but of me allowing myself to get carried away into old patterns.

But here's what I saw when I looked back at this story with my mindfulness tools and with an eye for red flags. The first red flag popped up within the first hour that I spent with Joel: that 'intense, coiled-up energy' that he radiated and my 'perma-grin.' In hindsight I can recognize that my body was reacting to his energy with a heightened sense of awareness. My body was actually in a fear state because of his emotional instability. I only interpreted it as excitement because of the patterning that I had developed in early childhood in relation to my sister. It stems from being a little girl whose closest relationship was with my older sister whom I loved intensely. My love for her was mixed with deep, almost constant fear that I would lose her attention and/or make her angry with me. She had that kind of intense energy inside her, too, and when she focused it on me, I felt loved and happy and special. When she got angry with me I felt like the sun had blown out and that it was all my fault. When she ignored me I felt like I was going to die, literally.[5] This relationship with my sister imprinted itself deeply into my psyche and became my

---

[5] I literally mean "literally." Studies suggest that the brain registers social rejection as similar to physical pain. See Kirsten Weir, "The pain of social rejection," *The Monitor* 43, no. 4 (April 2012), accessed April 20, 2019, https://www.apa.org/monitor/2012/04/rejection.aspx.

model for what I understood love to feel like. The type of love that was familiar and comfortable for me was love that was like a faulty faucet: always either turned on full blast or shut off completely. I went on to recreate that dynamic in all my romantic relationships: picking men who I later found out had alcoholic, manic-depressive, and/or narcissistic tendencies. If by chance I met someone who didn't fit this profile and wanted to love me in any healthy way, I ran fast as fuck away because that was too scary.

Why was it scary? Because my psyche did not recognize actual love *as love* to me. I would question their motives, feel less safe around them than I did with the narcissistic, manic-depressive alcoholics.

I can now recognize that my body on high alert is actually signaling me to be careful, that a mentally unstable person is nearby. But even when I learned this truth about myself, after deep, intense work with a therapist, I continued to choose the same type of men for a long time. I met Joel when I had already been in therapy for a few years. But those darn grooves in my brain equated love with constantly striving to win the love of someone who was emotionally and mentally unavailable most of the time.

I believe this is quite a common pattern in our culture, reflected and reinforced in our entertainment and is unfortunately emphasized by a lot of our media. The idea of "love at first sight," and "being struck by lightning" is the plot of millions of films, love songs, and novels and teaches us to seek out that rush of adrenaline. It's rare to see a story like *Frozen* (which apparently relates to a lot of my life) where Anna, who initially falls head over heels with a handsome prince who finishes her sandwiches, eventually discovers that she should have paid more attention to the red flags.

I want to be crystal clear here: I am not placing blame on myself or anyone else. I am not saying, "Poor me, I dated narcissists," or, "Poor me, I have a sister with serious mental health issues who ignored me as a child." We are all doing the best we can. We are all working with and against the grooves in our brains, trying to use the often imperfect tools we were given by imperfect parents. I am here not to judge or to complain but rather to share the tools that I have learned and developed through years of intense study, practice, and coaching that have freed me and my clients from old patterns. They will allow you to make different choices in your romantic relationships and begin to change the grooves in your brain.

6

CONSTANT VIGILANCE!

One of the most invaluable tools is being able to pay attention to your body's signals and to stay open and present to what people show you about who they are as often as possible. Being present and aware of what your loved ones are saying and doing in every moment might just be the "secret sauce" to having healthy relationships — with your kids, your family, your lover.

How and why do we need to be present and "hold space" for our loved ones? You have to see them, hear them, and accept them exactly as they are, not as you want or expect or believe them to be. Recognize your own projections, your own triggers, and your own stories as they come up. You have to allow your loved ones to show you who they are because if you do not, then they will not receive what they need and want in the relationship. And you will not be living in truth. Instead you will be living and operating under a delusion and that leads directly into feelings of hurt, betrayal, and rejection.

Please recognize that I am not saying you have to like or agree with everything someone says or does. That would be impossible anyway. I am saying to let go, as much as you can, of pretending and wishing things were different in that moment. Let go of creating stories in your head about why they are acting a certain way. If you don't understand a loved one's choice, be clear and honest about that. Ask them "why" instead of assuming you know.

A few weeks ago I had an experience with a close friend that illustrates the value of speaking my truth when I feel hurt by a loved one. I needed someone to pick my kids up from school and watch them for most of the evening while I attended a fundraiser event. I knew my friend Angelique babysits occasionally so I told her what I needed and asked her what her rates were. She told me $25/hour for two kids. I felt shocked in the moment at the high cost but didn't say anything. I got off the phone with her and proceeded to stew over this situation the rest of the day — *Why would she charge me such a high rate?! I can't pay that! We're friends! I just did her a big favor and I thought she would want to do me a favor back!*

Thankfully, I cleared my head enough the following day to remember that we are close friends and that a better choice in this situation was to speak to her directly and ask her, "Why didn't you offer to do me a favor and watch my kids?" Her response was simple and, in retrospect, quite obvious. I had not asked her for a favor. I asked her what her rates were as a babysitter, so she told me. She went on to explain that she thought I just wanted to know her rates and had expected for us to continue to discuss the situation from there. She said, "If you had asked me for a favor I would have most likely said, 'Of course!' You can trust me to be clear with what I am willing to do and not do." If I had not had the courage to ask Angelique directly about why she had behaved in a way that made me feel hurt, our friendship would have suffered unnecessarily.

You have now learned the first stage on your journey towards healthy, joyful relationships. It begins by first focusing on filling your relationship with yourself with greater acceptance and trust. You practice presence and hold space for all parts of yourself — all your resistance, challenging emotions, and protector parts. You call a truce in your battle against the parts of yourself that make you feel uncomfortable in any way, taking a break from self-criticism. You then walk these practices outwards into your relationships with your friends, family, children, and romantic partners. You remember to hold space for each important person in your life — seeing, hearing and accepting them for who they are in that moment. The more you can listen to yourself and your loved ones, without judgment, assumptions, or wishing the situation was different, the more stable and empowered you will feel and the more your life and your relationships will be filled with ease and joy.

PART TWO

EXPAND COMPASSION & TRUST

Part One covered the basics of practicing presence and learning to accept all the parts of yourself and others.. In Part Two, you will take the next step in your journey out of the old, muddy ruts and into healthy, joyful, peaceful relationships by expanding your compassion for yourself and your loved ones. This next step is more challenging as it requires you to acknowledge and forgive yourself for anything in your past about which you feel shame or regret. Your trust and love for yourself will deepen exponentially as you go through this part of your journey.

    I will again draw a parallel between how you build a new friendship and how you improve your relationship with yourself. You have spent some time getting to know yourself, accepting all the parts of yourself without judgment. Now, how do you go beyond acceptance and presence to the trust that allows you to take risks and the compassion that helps you recover from missteps? Think about how you have come to really trust a new person in your life. With some people, it probably felt pretty quick and easy. You discovered similarities and common values and just clicked. With others it probably took years of running into one another at parties or hanging out in groups.

One well-documented situation that is known to build trust is when people experience a challenging, frightening, or harrowing situation together. Think of group survival stories: soldiers in battle, refugees in transit, people displaced by storms. Think of how, after 9/11, New Yorkers reached out and helped one another despite and within their own vulnerability and fear. They forged long-lasting bonds of trust, compassion, and understanding very quickly because of the vulnerability their shared experience created and because of they way they reacted to that vulnerability.

You can form those same bonds of trust, compassion, and understanding *with yourself* when you are present with your pain. You prove to yourself that no matter the circumstances you can trust yourself, and you expand your capacity for compassion both for yourself and all your loved ones.

7

PRACTICING PRESENCE WITH YOUR PAIN

In this section we will focus on practicing presence with emotional pain specifically. Practicing presence with physical pain resulting from an injury or physical ailment, although possible, is beyond my expertise and beyond the scope of this book. *Emotional* pain comes from our interpretation or experience of an event rather than a physical cause. That said, emotional pain is most often accompanied by physical symptoms, even though nothing is directly acting on your nerve endings. When you read about the tragic death of a child in the newspaper, for example, you may feel a pain in your chest, but there is no physical ailment causing this. When you feel pain from missing someone you love, whether it's after a breakup or a death, it can feel overwhelming — you may ache all over or feel like you have to vomit. It can feel like someone is stabbing you in the heart.

When we don't know how to hold our emotional pain, we generally learn to hide it, numb it, or run from it. None of these solutions changes the pain, and none of them makes the pain truly go away. What's extra wonderful about choosing to hold yourself through your emotional pain is that you can actually begin to diminish that pain. When you sit with your pain, accept that it is a part of you in that moment, you begin to realize that a large part of the pain comes not from the situation itself but from the stories and meaning you attach to it.

Try this exercise to begin being present to your pain. Remember or imagine a situation in which you have felt heartbroken such as hearing a song on the radio that reminds you of a lost lover. What do you feel in your body? Do you feel physical pain in your chest? Your throat? Your belly? Before the break up, that same song brought you joy. Has the song changed? Of course not. In fact, I believe that the emotional response the song triggers has also not changed; what has changed is the story your mind creates about it.

Let's look at this more closely. Hearing the song when your relationship felt strong and solid triggers your mind to respond with thoughts such as, *I love this song. It makes me so happy because it reminds me of Harry (let's call him Harry) and how we love each other so much. Life is so wonderful!* When you hear the song after the break up and you feel lonely and rejected, you may have thoughts such as, *Life is so shitty. Why did Harry leave me?! Poor me. This hurts so much! Why does this station play this song so often?*

Interestingly, the actual physical sensations that you feel in both cases are usually quite similar: a warm, throbbing sensation in your chest. The first time, feeling that warmth in your chest triggers additional feelings of love, safety, and belonging. The second time the feeling of warmth triggers feelings of hurt, betrayal, sadness. The reason they are similar sensations are that they both contain an element of love. The difference is in the meaning or stories you attach to those sensations in different circumstances. Thus, the key to changing your pain is to shift the stories you tell yourself in moments of pain. Over time, you can lessen the intensity of the pain you feel in your body as you reframe the emotional significance of it.

How do you change these stories? The first step is to shift how you look at the nature of relationships in general and get clear on what expectations and conditioning you have been unconsciously attaching to your relationships. Casting a critical eye at the stories that so many of us have told ourselves after the ending of a romantic relationship is a perfect place to start. Even when a relationship was short-lived, there is often some version of, *What's wrong with me? What did I do wrong?* Or, *All men suck/All women are shallow.* When you can take a step back and look logically at the situation, however it becomes quite evident how erroneous these stories are. How would it feel if you consciously created new stories in your head to tell yourself after a break up such as,

> *I learned what I needed to from this relationship. This relationship is over now, but that does not erase the wonderful moments of connection and love I felt during it. I now have an opportunity to comfort and soothe myself in this time of pain. I now have an opportunity to receive love and support from dear friends.*

The next time you are aware of feeling strong emotional pain, take a moment to ask yourself, *What story am I telling myself right now? What meaning am I attaching to this experience?* Just that step alone begins to create a bit of distance from the story and allows you to reframe your reactions.

8

REFRAMING PAIN

But pain hurts! your internal protectors will scream out. They will push you away from the pain, encourage you to ignore it, numb it, or turn it outwards into anger. And where do such choices lead? Only to more pain. To feeling powerless, to feeling overwhelmed by external forces in your life, and to having less respect for yourself. If you've had a history of damaging relationships, then your protectors have learned a story that keeps you safe(-ish) but that closes you off from real intimacy and trust with yourself or others. You need to shift the stories you tell not only about your experiences but about what role pain plays in your life.

Pain can be a teacher, for instance. Of course, it is never desirable, but that does not mean we should avoid any situation with a risk of causing us pain. I would put it even more strongly and argue that pain is, in fact, a necessary and even valuable part of life. Think of how children learn to avoid touching a hot stove. They touch one for the first time and burn their fingers. The pain sends an immediate signal to their brain to pull their hand away. They then seek comfort: put their fingers in their mouths, hug themselves, and cry for mom or dad. The pain of a burned hand becomes an opportunity for a child to learn not only to avoid hot stoves but how to care for him- or herself and how to seek out comfort from loved ones when in distress.

Would you really know how to love yourself deeply — through all of the highs and lows of this wild human existence — without pain as a teacher?

Pain can also be a catalyst for changing your life. When everything in your life is going well and you feel amazing all the time, do you want to change anything? It is only when you suffer that you understand that something has to shift in order to feel better, to make things better. Recognize that if you are suffering now, then now is the time for you to change.

I want to be crystal clear here: I am not saying, "Everything happens for a reason, so don't try to change anything." I'm also absolutely *not* saying that you deserve the pain you are feeling. Many people, especially women, stay in a painful relationship or situation because they believe things like that. I believe we have choices about how to react to and respond to whatever life throws at you and in that way we can deepen our acceptance, trust, and love for ourselves, which in turn fills your life with way more joy and pleasure.

At the same time, I do believe that if you choose to love other people, you *will* experience pain and suffering; it's part of the package. The point is that you are not a hopeless victim simply because you experience pain; you get to choose how you respond to those painful moments. You get to choose how you respond to other humans. You can choose to use the pain as a catalyst to strengthen your self-love or allow it to push you in the other direction, away from yourself, towards fear, numbness, anger, and regret.

What happens when you let yourself sink into your pain and feel all the sadness, hurt, grief, regret, and loneliness inside you? Allowing these painful emotions to flood through your whole system will hurt — *a lot*. Not only that, it is intensely frightening, too. But eventually something amazing happens: you come out the other side of it. You survive it. You learn that emotional pain does not last forever. Just as, one way or another, all relationships come to an end, so too will your emotional pain. Fully appreciating this fact alone will diminish the pain, because part of the power of pain is actually not the sadness, loneliness, or grief itself — it's the fear that the suffering will never end.

I remember once telling my therapist that I was afraid to let myself feel sad. She was encouraging me, in the session, to let myself cry for all the ways I had been hurt throughout my life by other people. I couldn't do it. I was afraid that if I started crying I would never stop. I had numbed myself from my sadness, covering it up with anger for so many years that it felt like a deep lake pushing against a dam. I believed that if I allowed a hole to form in the dam, let even a little trickle of sadness through, the weight of the whole lake would burst through explosively and drown me. My therapist helped me to see that damming up the pain actually made it more powerful and more likely to negatively impact my life forever. The only way to diminish emotional pain is to allow yourself to actually experience it fully. You will find that it will run its natural course through you and, eventually, out of you.

The irrefutable truth about life is that nothing lasts forever, no matter what the fairy tales teach us. When you go into all your close relationships knowing that simple fact, you experience much less pain down the line. Holding and comforting yourself when you are experiencing painful emotions is an incredible tool for increasing your self-love, as well as saving you from the often-debilitating fear that the pain will last forever. The most basic truth to know about close, devoted relationships is that they will not be easy. Whether your attachment is with family, lovers, spouses or children, at some point there will be pain. At some point the relationship will end. The one irrefutable fact of human existence is that we are not immortal; at some point, we all die. (The question of the immortality of the soul, which I find fascinating, is a matter for another day.) What we can all agree on is that we exist in our bodies right now, for this one lifetime. So why, for the love of all that's holy, do the vast majority of us choose to ignore that fact on a daily basis? Why do we let pain bind us and bad patterns keep us mired in mud, poisoning our few years on this earth?

My dear Aunt Sherrie died earlier this year after being married to my uncle for almost 50 years. They had a great life together and many years of happiness. My uncle feels gratitude that her physical suffering is over and that she is at peace, but he is suffering from almost bottomless sadness and pain because he misses her. We all miss her: she was an amazing person that lit up the hearts of everyone who knew her. We will all miss her presence in our lives for the rest of our lives. The ache in our hearts will always be present, but so will the feelings of love we have when sharing our memories of her with one another. Would my uncle, because of the grief he is now feeling, wish away the previous 50 years of his marriage? I don't think so.

9

OVERCOMING SHAME WITH INTEGRITY

Now that you have begun the process of building up compassion and trust in yourself by reframing your emotional pain and learning to accept it, it's time to tackle one of the most difficult stretches on your journey toward building a stable core of self trust and self love: facing the parts of yourself that you have been ignoring because of shame and guilt. In order to have the healthy, joyful, sustainable relationships you deserve, you first have to take responsibility for and forgive yourself for the times when your actions have been out of sync with your values or otherwise lacked integrity.[6]

A person builds his/her integrity when they get closer to a state of wholeness in themselves, living in alignment with their personal morals and ethical principles. This means acknowledging and taking responsibility for the parts of you

---

[6] My understanding of the word *integrity* incorporates two definitions from Dictionary.com:
1. *Adherence to moral and ethical principles; soundness of moral character; honesty.*
2. *Adherence to the state of being whole, entire, or undiminished.*

that you are least proud of. This is challenging: you may feel vulnerable, weak, and/or ashamed.

The good news is that facing your weaknesses and out-of-integrity moments is the surest way to learn from them and grow past them. Simply acknowledging the existence of those parts of you that you feel shame about will diminish their power. Unacknowledged, these shadow parts wield undue influence on you; they may even trick you into thinking that they *are* you. When you allow these parts out into the light, open and identified, you are able to see them for what they are: part of you, but not all of you. You have the courage to do this, trust me — or you would not have gotten this far on your journey.

When you build a strong internal foundation of integrity, your check-ins become easier. You can remember that you, like everybody else in the universe, are not perfect. You are a complex mix of a dazzling array of different parts: including compassion, courage, light, and joy. You will be reminded that the shadow parts (anger, fear, resentment, etc.) do not define you. The more you pretend that certain emotions don't exist inside you, the more powerful they become. It is almost impossible to forgive yourself and move past the emotions you are ashamed of until you acknowledge them. Remember that if a good friend exhibited those emotions or acted without integrity you would still love them and forgive them easily. Have the same compassion for yourself. The more you can acknowledge all the parts of yourself, the less power shame and guilt have over you and thus the stronger your integrity becomes. The more you act with integrity, the more joyful, healthy and easy your relationships will feel.

Imagine a tired father yells at his infant daughter when she wakes up crying in the middle of the night. The next morning he feels guilt and shame for his reaction. He loves his daughter deeply and wants to always treat her with kindness and compassion. His rational brain knows that she did nothing wrong; she is an infant who only knows how to get her needs met by crying. In that moment of fatigue, though, neither his loving, compassionate heart nor his rational brain was in charge.

Was he acting in alignment with his personal morals and values? Of course not. He was acting from a place of frustration, tiredness, and resentment. Perhaps the crying also triggered feelings of helplessness and failure because he didn't know how to help her fall back asleep.

How can this father close the gaps in his integrity? How can he recover from not living up to his own morals and values? First he has to acknowledge to himself that he was not acting from a place of integrity. He then might want to show his infant daughter extra love and attention the next morning. He might think about how he and his partner could support each other better to shoulder the responsibility of caring for their daughter. He can question what caused him to lose his temper in that situation. If it had been an older child, he could apologize for his behavior.

The point is that you have to *take responsibility* for your lapses in judgment in order to build up your moral strength, courage, and wholeness. This is how you close those gaps. With practice you will be able to choose how you act and react in situations that normally trigger you. The ability to do this is a life-changer and a relationship-transformer.

Now think about an experience in your life that made you feel burning-hot, nauseating shame. As I mentioned in the introduction, one of the most debilitating moments of shame in my life was when I admitted that my marriage was over. I kept thinking, *I'm a failure. I should've worked harder. I should've pushed my husband to work harder. My children will be traumatized and it's my fault.*

How did I heal? The first stage of healing came from understanding, acknowledging, and accepting responsibility for my role in the failed marriage. I came to understand that the end of a marriage, or any relationship for that matter, does not necessarily mean one or both people failed. Sometimes (not always) two people grow and change and need different things. Sometimes the problem is that people don't grow and change. Eventually I realized that assigning blame wasn't helpful, while acceptance was. Marriages fail. Humans fail. Perhaps I failed, but that failure does not define me as a failure. I failed at this one thing.

A second stage of healing came when I changed my mindset around failing. Just as I had to reframe pain as my body telling me about my experience, I had to reframe failure. To begin with, I realized failure does not have to be something to feel ashamed of. The only people who never fail are those who never try anything new. This is a lesson I find myself having to teach my children perhaps more than any other. We make it a regular practice at the dinner table to each say something that we failed at that day. With this practice I am encouraging them to reframe their failures as a cause for celebration. Failure shows you your path towards growth and learning. It gives you the opportunity to build your integrity by acknowledging your failures, asking for forgiveness if necessary, and being authentically vulnerable. Your biggest failures in life are the greatest opportunities to learn and the strongest instigators for you to break out of old patterns.

10

TAKING RESPONSIBILITY FOR YOUR EMOTIONS

A huge plus of acknowledging and accepting all the parts of yourself — including your painful emotions and failures — is that you begin to take responsibility for them yourself rather than putting the responsibility and blame for them on your loved ones. Why is this beneficial?

In order to answer this, let's look at what happens when, falling into old habits, you choose to do the opposite and believe that any and all feelings of love, safety, and acceptance that you experience can only be triggered by someone outside yourself such as a loved one, friend, parent, sibling, or even child.

You know at least three negative consequences usually follow from this:

1. **You give away your personal power.** When you believe that someone else controls your feelings, you are giving them power over you. You are the sovereign king or queen of your own self — your feelings, emotions, thoughts, actions, and reactions.
2. **You become enmeshed.** You may hear people talk about this as "codependence," but I don't much like

that term, personally. I think the word *codependent* actually sounds too much like *interdependence*, which is a good thing. In interdependence, two people depend on each other or trust each other to each be their own sovereign person, taking responsibility for themselves. A clearer term for relying on others for your emotional life is *enmeshed*. To me, that creates the feeling and image of two people who have lost their clear, healthy boundaries and are entangled with each other. Entanglement and a lack of healthy boundaries will always lead to resentment and suffering.

3. **You lose integrity.** You cut yourself off from parts of yourself, thus operating from fractured parts of yourself instead of from your whole, grounded self.

For many years I shaped my life around other people: shutting down parts of myself and relinquishing my authentic power and integrity under the mistaken belief that this was how to keep me safe, loved, and accepted. This path in some ways did keep me safe: safe from my own fears, shadows, failures, and inadequacies. I had learned somewhere in life that my emotions were dangerous and something to shove out of sight. This caused me to feel unable to handle them, to fear my own emotions. Codependency or enmeshment felt safer and more comfortable to me because it kept my focus outward; I didn't have to face my frightening inner world.

When you are enmeshed like that, you stop believing and trusting in yourself. You experience life as a puppet on your loved one's string. You can fall easily into a victimhood mentality and lose all connection to your personal power. After that there are basically three options: cut yourself off from all feelings and live life as much as possible from your mind, spend most of your life finding ways to hide from your emotions through any number of numbing behaviors, or look for different people in your life to handle your feelings for you.

Unfortunately, two of these options are popular pop culture narratives these days. Many narratives center on the search for "the one" who will make the hero's or heroine's life complete.

I offer a fourth way to deal with difficult emotions and handle pain in your life that allows you to claim your own authentic power, act with integrity, and build healthy, joyful relationships. When you can handle your own emotions and learn to ride the waves of emotions like a fearless surfer, you become powerful, free, and joyful in all areas of your life, including relationships.

To see how taking responsibility for your own emotions can affect intimate relationships, let's return to the fictional relationship with Harry. Let's suppose that you and Harry are in a healthy relationship and you're listening to "your song," but this time you are aware that (a) you are loved, safe, and accepted at all times and (b) no relationships last forever. [7]You are holding each other, dancing together, feeling completely happy and peaceful. You are thinking, *What a beautiful night. I will never forget this magical moment.* But now you understand that although you feel completely in love with Harry, your feelings exist in your body and are being generated by you. They don't all depend upon Harry or the song or anything else. You remember that you can feel those pleasurable emotions any time you choose. You are not being cynical; you are simply being present to your emotions, and by taking responsibility for them you are able to avoid creating unrealistic expectations for them. You may feel complete love for Harry and at the same time remember that your feelings of love, safety, and acceptance are not dependent on him.

Imagine now that you break up with Harry, and sometime later you hear "your song." You experience a messy hodgepodge

---

[7] I am not being morbid here; I am being realistic. Even if Harry's and your love lasts 50-plus years, there is no guarantee he will not die before you.

of emotions: sadness, loneliness, anger, regret, and maybe even fear of never finding another healthy relationship. Now imagine staying with those feelings for the moment without pushing them away or attaching shame or fear of the future to them.

Accepting your more challenging feelings, creates a bit of internal space to experience again the love you felt for Harry. Remember that you are always accepted no matter what; even if you are stranded on a desert island for the rest of your life, you are always accepted by yourself. This may even allow some feelings of gratitude to surface — for the moments of pleasure, joy, and connection that you shared with Harry. Even if you do not yet feel genuine gratitude, sadness and other painful emotions lessen when you stay grounded in self-acceptance without judgment.

Once I was able to look at my life and all my decisions as opportunities to learn and build integrity in myself, I gained an enormous amount of wisdom and confidence. When I learned to acknowledge and forgive myself for my failures, I found an ease and freedom in my life and compassion for my loved ones. I was able to understand, accept, and have compassion for failures and other undesirable qualities in other people the more I understood and accepted those parts in myself.

Our harshest reactions, after all, are usually directed at those people that remind us of parts of ourselves that we are secretly most ashamed of. Triggers differ from person to person, but we all have them and we all have a unique way of reacting to them. We are each born with certain personality traits and predilections that make us more susceptible to favoring certain parts and ignoring other parts of ourselves. Other forces can also exert a powerful influence on your actions and reactions, in addition to your natural personality traits. Parents, friends, religion, life experiences, social media, and society in general all contribute to our emotional integrity and affect how well we relate to all parts of ourselves and what kinds of experiences trigger us.

One of my triggers is witnessing laziness in people, especially when other folks around them are working hard. I am, in general, a pretty calm, even-keeled person. Whether it's because I am a Taurus or have low blood pressure, who knows. I have enormous patience for people who are new to a task and timid to try or have issues that make it difficult for them to accomplish something in particular, but lazy people? *Oof!* I tend to crack the proverbial whip. (Just ask the many people who worked or volunteered for me when I ran the free meal program in Poughkeepsie, NY.)

I will probably never be completely free of this impatience, but by understanding that everyone, myself included, does not always operate at his or her best (and that this may sometimes include being — or appearing — lazy), I was able to admit a little bit of compassion into my psyche. Moreover, I discovered my own fear of being perceived as lazy, and when I faced this, it freed me from the burden of keeping that fear buried deep inside myself and constantly working to fool others. I wasted so much time and energy for so long.

Now I know that if there are people who see me as lazy, there is not much I can do about it. And in fact, they are a little bit right. Most of the time I work very hard — raising my kids, coaching, writing, exercising, maintaining my house. But I have lazy times too. Sometimes I succeed in my goals and sometimes I fail. If someone's taking the time to judge me, based on those times, then that says more about them than about me. Perhaps he/she is afraid of facing his/her own shame and shadow parts. Dealing with my own shameful parts has allowed me to recognize the commonalities we share as fallible human beings and enabled me to feel compassion for those who judge me. This ability alone is worth all the hundreds of hours I've spent on self-acceptance work.

11

THE COURAGE TO BE VULNERABLE

Taking responsibility for your own feelings — whether pleasurable or painful — is a crucial step in having healthy, joyful relationships with your loved ones. Once you take responsibility for your emotions and failures, you now face another difficult task. Now you must work on allowing yourself to be seen by your loved ones authentically and vulnerably.

What is vulnerability? Brené Brown, an expert on vulnerability and shame, says this in *Daring Greatly:*

> I define vulnerability as uncertainty, risk, and emotional exposure. With that definition in mind, let's think about love. Waking up every day and loving someone who may or may not love us back, whose safety we can't ensure, who may stay in our lives or may leave without a moment's notice, who may be loyal to the day they die or betray us tomorrow — that's vulnerability. Love is uncertain. It's incredibly risky. And loving someone leaves us emotionally exposed. Yes, it's scary, and yes, we're open to being hurt, but can you imagine your life without loving or being loved?

Choosing close, loving relationships requires you to be vulnerable in so many ways. Just as you need to hold space for your loved ones to be their authentic selves, so too do you have to show up as your authentic, vulnerable self. You have to voice your needs, your fears, and your heart's desires. You have to recognize the times in your life when your integrity has lapsed and you have acted out of fear or shame. You have to let yourself feel conflicting emotions and accept that the truth in most situations is complicated and nuanced. Allowing a loved one to see you in your authentic, vulnerable truth is an incredibly important cornerstone of building healthy, joyful, sustainable relationships.

Sometimes, when I ponder vulnerability, I think about my cat, Peanut. He constantly demands attention, love, and affection but is regularly rejected. Even as I write these words he is nudging my arm, trying to get me to pet him rather than type. I reject him many times a day. He does not seem bothered, however. He does not go hide in a corner, nursing his bruised ego. He does not react in anger, growling or scratching to punish me for not giving him what he wants. He never seems to make up stories to explain why I didn't pet him: *Maybe my fur isn't soft enough. Maybe I need a bigger butt. Or a smaller butt, then she will love me. Maybe I'm too needy, I'll play hard to get and then she will love me.*

When I push him away he either lies down next to me, purring, or finds a soft spot elsewhere in the house to nap. He does not seem to take my rejection personally, and he never stops demanding attention and affection from me (and every other human he meets). I know I am anthropomorphizing, here; I don't know what my cat is feeling. However, in the 15 years he has lived with me, he has never stopped seeking and demanding affection, which strongly suggests that he is not afraid of rejection despite experiencing a mixture of both rejection and acceptance.

Does he know in that little cat brain that I love him? Does he feel worthy and deserving of my love and affection? Is he filled with deep self-love? Who knows? It is not my goal to try to unravel the inner workings of my cat's psyche. I only use him as an example to highlight by contrast a common, though unfortunate, human behavior: allowing our own sense of worthiness to depend on another person's affection and love for us. We could all learn a little something from our cats.

My relationship with Peanut highlights another important truth about how humans relate to others. Note that my decision to pet him or ignore him always stems from how I am feeling or what I am doing in that moment. When I am writing and he plops down on top of my computer, I push him off. If I am relaxing on the couch, watching a movie with my kids, I welcome his warm furry body on my lap. I do not love him more or differently at the time that I give him what he wants than at the time that I reject him. And just like situational factors determine whether I respond to him, situational factors impact the people in your life, too. When you feel rejected, you do not need to conclude that this person will never want you around again. Sometimes the message is just, "I'm sorry, but now is not a great time for me."

So, what can we learn from Peanut about having the resilience to be vulnerable? The first important point is that Peanut has a well-stocked pleasure treasure chest. (We will get to this in the next section.) When I choose not to pet him, even though that is his favorite thing in the world, he will go find pleasure elsewhere — his favorite sunny spot on the couch or another human in the house. More importantly, though, is that he seems to have a very clear sense of his own self-worth. He doesn't take my rejection of him personally. He may not like it, but it doesn't seem to change how he feels about himself. Peanut asks for what he wants every day, because why shouldn't he? What else is he doing with his life?

His whole life is about taking care of himself, making sure his needs get met.

Your life is not that different. Yes, it's more complicated — with jobs, money, politics, families, etc., but underneath it all, we are all driven by a desire to be safe, loved, and appreciated by the people we trust, and we want to provide love and safety to those same people. Even if you argue that your life is about being a good person, perhaps helping others, (which I often argue, myself) I believe that underneath that are the same desires. Why do you want to be a good person and help others? Because you want to be loved — maybe by God, maybe by your parents, or maybe both. Or maybe you want to get to heaven — you believe that being a good person and helping others will keep you safe from eternal damnation. Whatever your personal beliefs are, the desires underneath are universal: to be safe, loved, and accepted for who you truly are.

Given this truth, it makes even more sense that you would feel terrified of being vulnerable, speaking your truth, and asking to be seen, heard, and loved. It is nothing less than your life's purpose; of course you are going to be extra sensitive to rejection in this area. So, please stop judging yourself for any fear and resistance you may feel about this kind of vulnerability. Instead, accept this fear as part of practicing presence with yourself, build up your internal sense of self and integrity, and then choose vulnerability anyway.

Now, you do need to be smart about the people you choose to be vulnerable with. We will discuss safety in vulnerability in the next chapter and how to discern when and with whom you choose to be vulnerable. Some people in your life will get triggered by your vulnerability and reject you. Other people will sometimes reject you and sometimes embrace you in your vulnerability. Overall though, the only way to build closer connections and create deeper bonds of love is through showing up in your authenticity and vulnerability.

Another universal truth that may encourage you to embrace vulnerability is that the more vulnerable you are with your emotions and needs, the more love you will receive. I do not mean that everyone in your life will love you more just because you show them love. Rather, the healthiest relationships you have will become richer and more fulfilling.

This is a truth that I have only recently understood myself and it has been life-changing. Surprisingly enough I got clarity about this from the children's film *Inside Out*. The main character, a young girl named Riley, is trying to navigate through all her conflicting feelings about her family's recent move to a new city. Her parents are dealing with the move themselves and are not paying close attention to how Riley is struggling. They tell her a few times how much they appreciate how happy she always is, how that helps them deal with all of the chaos in their lives. She interprets her parents' words to mean that she shouldn't show them any unhappy feelings about the move or even allow herself to feel sad.

Finally, at the end of the film, she shares her feelings with her parents authentically and vulnerably. In response, her parents share that they also feel sad sometimes in the new city and they comfort her with hugs and words of love, support, and affection.

I remember the first few times I saw this film (as a mom, I tend to see my kids' favorite films over and over), I did not understand the lesson being taught. That is, I understood logically what the movie was saying — that in order for Riley to feel happier, she had to allow herself to feel sad and share that emotion with her parents — but I didn't understand what that meant. I didn't understand why feeling sad and sharing that with loved ones would help me, because I was so used to hiding from my own vulnerable feelings of sadness from fear of rejection. After many viewings of the film and a ton of self-inquiry work, I finally comprehended the truth: if you hide your vulnerability from your loved ones, it creates separation and distance in that relationship. Just as we learned that hiding your vulnerable emotions from yourself, creates internal separation between different parts of yourself.

It is also useful to remember that your particular areas of vulnerability are unique to you; certain things will trigger a fear of vulnerability in you that won't trigger other people. Pay attention to your personal signals and allow them to point you in the direction of growth and stronger connection with people. For example, many people feel shy and vulnerable about dancing in public. Feelings of self-judgment and awkwardness come up; often there are stories such as "My body looks weird" and "I look foolish." For me though dancing in front of people is smack in the middle of my comfort zone. I feel completely at ease when dancing and couldn't care less how I look to other people.

I feel quite vulnerable and scared though when sharing my writing with other people. When I am alone, writing, I feel confident in the wisdom I share and in my ability to express it through words. Every time I go to share a document with a friend or family member, however, I feel immediate tightness in my throat and constriction in my chest. My mind tells me really extreme stories along the lines of, *This is garbage! Nobody needs to read this! You seriously thought this was a worthwhile use of your time?! Get a job! Stop playing around with this nonsense! Do NOT share this with ANYONE! They will think you are a fool and a jerk.*

Seriously, I am not exaggerating.

Thankfully, I now have the tools to hold myself with love and compassion during these hateful barrages from my inner protectors (remember — they are just attempting to protect me from hurt, rejection and ridicule.) Now, I am able to share my writing with people I trust. I also share my fears too by saying, "This is scary for me. I want your honest feedback and please say it with gentleness and love." The people I share my honest feelings with feel honored and grateful that I trust them; our relationship is strengthened and our bond deepens.

Leaning into your fear and vulnerability is incredibly healing because it creates new neural pathways in your head that strengthen over time with practice. The new narratives in your head will be a version of, *I can do this. I survived that scary experience,* and *People like my writing (or art, dancing, signing, etc.). It's safe to share. It's safe to be vulnerable.*

Choosing vulnerability has a snowball effect in your psyche — building up your courage, creating more internal confidence and self-trust, and opening up space for you to take on even bigger and potentially scarier challenges.

12

RISKING VULNERABILITY ... WISELY

Every time you choose vulnerability, you risk feeling hurt and rejected. Numerous scientific studies have established that rejection by a loved one can feel to your nervous system like dying. So, why would you risk this pain? Doesn't it make sense to keep yourself safe from those feelings? Shouldn't you listen to your body's reactions? If it's saying this is scary, should you not work to make yourself feel safe? Aren't there times and people with whom it is not safe to be vulnerable?

Good questions! I love that you are thinking more from a place of connection to your body and its sensations. It's true that, because vulnerability is risky, you must learn to risk vulnerability wisely. This is an area in which we have to look more closely at what your body is actually reacting to.

We can look at the previous example of feeling vulnerable to share my writing: how I fear that people I love, respect, and trust will think I am a fool and a self-absorbed jerk. The sensations I feel in those moments are intense: my heart pounds, there's nausea in my throat and a strong urge to go and hide under the blanket. Why so dramatic? Because humans' nervous systems are unfortunately wired to equate rejection by our tribe with physical death. My nervous system feels the fear of rejection by my peers and equates that with death.

If I take the time to examine this fear, I quickly realize my brain is working from a false equation. My fear reaction when I share my writing is not based in the reality of the moment; it's based in a former reality that lives in my DNA and that I may never have experienced myself in this lifetime. When I stop to consider the other truths in that situation, what do I uncover? The people with whom I share my writing love, respect, and trust me. That's why we have a close relationship. They will love, respect and trust me, regardless of what they think about my writing. No matter how they react to my writing, I am still safe and loved in my life. If, after I was vulnerable with them, one of these people all of a sudden thinks I am a jerk, then I probably don't want them in my life anymore.

Let's dig deeper into this example. What if I share my writing with a loved one and they express that they still love me, but they think what I have written is crap? Part of my brain wants to react almost as strongly as if they thought *I* was a piece of crap. But let's slow down and give them the benefit of the doubt. Let's ask, why do they think it's crap? There are three likely answers:

1. They think the writing is not good enough and that I can do better. This reaction stems out of deep love and respect for me and their belief that I have so much to offer to readers.
2. They think that writing is not the best way for me to share my gifts with the world: that I should find a different path. This reaction also stems from a deep love and respect for me and the desire for me to be happy and fulfilled in life.
3. They're not actually talking about the quality of the writing, but instead something in it triggers uncomfortable feelings in them such as anger, shame, fear,

and vulnerability, and they are only able to express this as criticism.

It is usually pretty easy to discern which of these three responses a reader is having just by consciously listening and observing them.

If they dislike my writing because of either of the first two reasons, they will most likely let me know that honestly. They might feel a bit shy with #2, but it is not too hard to figure out the meaning underneath their kind but not so supportive words. If I receive a response of anger, dismissiveness, jealousy, or derision from someone that I know loves and respects me, then there is no question they have been triggered somehow and the best choice for me is to try not to take it personally.

I would try not to take it personally, but I would not pretend that it hadn't occurred. I would not ignore their reaction because that would lead to possibly having that experience with that person over and over. You do not need to torture yourself by repeatedly seeking help, approval, validation, etc. from someone who is incapable of giving it to you in that particular area. Take the experience as useful information for yourself going forward: that person is not safe to share this part of yourself with authenticity and vulnerability, unless something shifts. You can be open to having a conversation with your friend or loved one about their reaction if they are aware enough and open to doing that with you.

The ability to share yourself with authenticity and vulnerability and to discern with whom and when it is safe to do so is something you can foster in your children from a very young age. As we model for them, by sharing our own vulnerable feelings, thoughts and fears, they learn that it is safe to be open with people that love them. They learn to expect that response from people they are close to and thereby not accept the opposite in their friends, potential partners and colleagues. I have a beautiful story to share here about how this worked for my daughter at a young age.

When Isadora was younger, she would often burst into tears when she was with me or her dad and her brother was not around. Her dad and I both originally took this to mean that she missed him. After a few months of her building up her courage to speak her truth, Isadora was able to share the feelings that were causing her to cry in those moments. Turns out, when Oliver was elsewhere, both her dad and I would wind up asking her a whole bunch of questions about what she wanted to do. We thought it was a "treat" for her to be the one in charge for a few hours: she could pick which books to read, what snacks we ate, etc.

But Izzy felt overwhelmed by the barrage of questions because she wasn't used to having to make so many decisions. At six years old, she did not know how to explain this to the loving grownups in her life and would therefore break down into tears. With patience on our parts, and courage on her part, we were able to figure it out eventually and she learned how to describe her vulnerable feelings with words.

A few weeks later I received a phone call from my mom sharing what has now become one of her favorite Izzy stories. My kids were spending the day with my folks. Oliver was playing chess with his grandpa and Izzy and my mom had just finished reading a book together. My mom then asked Izzy what she wanted to do next, "Pick another book? Draw a picture? Play cats? Go outside ... ?"

Izzy replied in a calm and confident voice, "Please don't overwhelm me, Gigi. I will let you know what I want to do next after I sit here for a minute doing nothing." My mom responded supportively and enthusiastically to this and Isadora learned that it was safe for her to speak her truth in this area with her grandma.

If my mom had responded differently and perhaps said something dismissive or derisive like, "What do you mean you feel overwhelmed?! I'm just asking you what you want to do!" or had responded in defensiveness with something like, "Fine! You don't want to be overwhelmed? I'll just leave and you can do whatever you like!" Izzy would have been hurt in the moment, of course, but would have learned a valuable lesson to be wary of her grandmother in future emotionally vulnerable situations.

It's also worth noting that people can learn how to respond to your vulnerability when you share your feelings. This is not a skill that most people learned from their parents nor is it taught in school. It's okay to take baby steps and to be patient with people and give them repeated opportunities to hold space for your vulnerability in a way that feels supportive to you.

I know it's a stereotype, but in my experience personally and through coaching, men do struggle more than women to learn vulnerability — but that doesn't mean they cannot learn it. Alison Armstrong's work has influenced me greatly in this realm, helping me to understand that *generally* when a man in my life fails to hold space for my vulnerable sharing of feelings, it is *not* because he doesn't care about me or thinks I am weak, stupid, or anything else problematic. His behavior in those moments results from a mix of his own conditioning about what it means to be a good man, his discomfort with his own vulnerable feelings, and his desire to provide for me by "fixing" my problem.

Diving too much further into these topics is a subject for another book, but please allow me a few more words on this subject here. People in general, and most men in particular, can learn how to hold space when they are helped to understand the value of the practice. This can be as simple as saying something like the following:

> My dear boyfriend — I want to talk with you about my feelings of grief and sadness around my aunt's death. The most helpful and supportive thing for me right now

would be for you to just listen to me with your loving heart. Advice and platitudes would not feel supportive to me right now. Having you lovingly hold space for me to share these feelings will provide an enormous feeling of safety for me. It will provide a feeling of relief from the burden of sadness and grief that I am carrying. Can you do that for me?

In this scenario, you do open yourself to the possibility that this person will say no. Demanding someone hold space for your feelings never leads to building more trust and intimacy in a relationship. If this is the first time you ask someone a question like this, he or she may say no almost automatically because it will feel like such a shock to their system and therefore will be frightening. Remember to not take this personally. Hold space for both of you in that moment. Their response, again as always, is coming from their own triggers and vulnerability.

And remember that demanding someone hold space for your feelings never leads to building more trust and intimacy in a relationship. Keep showing up, asking for what you need without demanding it and creating space for the other person to handle their own triggers and step up for you. And keep paying attention to your own needs, desires and triggers. Anyone who tries to learn this skill will eventually succeed — I guarantee it.

13

WHEN VULNERABILITY HURTS

There will be some people who cannot ever learn a master-ninja relationship skill such as this because they are too emotionally scarred and shut-down to attempt it. This is most unfortunate for them but also unfortunate for you if you love them. At a certain point, after a number of attempts on your part to ask for what you want and not get it, you will have to face the truth that that person simply cannot give you what you want. This is incredibly useful information. It may cause feelings of sadness, disappointment, and regret, but it's better for you to face that reality than to live in a fantasy. That will only lead to more sadness, disappointment, and regret down the line. When you face the truth, you can then decide how to respond to that information given your needs, values, and commitment to living with authenticity and integrity.

Sometimes being vulnerable means speaking your truth when you know it will disappoint or hurt someone you love. Have you ever found out a loved one has been lying to you? I know for me the hardest part is looking back over the past and realizing that the loved one was lying through it all: the sense of betrayal is immense and I feel like a total idiot.

This is especially true with romantic partners and parents. Parents have such high expectations and often think of their children as the most amazing people in the world, right? So, admitting to your parents that you've messed up or failed in some way can be especially vulnerable. With romantic partners, speaking your truth can often lead to hurt or pain when it's something that you need that they are not providing for you or when you feel hurt or disappointed by them in some meaningful way. This is opening yourself up in a different way — instead of getting hurt yourself, it's stepping into the possibility of hurting someone that you love.

Just as you learned that choosing love means choosing to experience pain sometimes, it also means choosing to *cause* pain sometimes. This can be an even harder pill to swallow and often requires even more courage than being vulnerable to being rejected or hurt yourself. As difficult as it is, it is 100% necessary for healthy, joyful, sustainable relationships.

As we've already seen, no relationships are static, things are always changing and shifting. And no matter how much we wish it weren't so, an important part of healthy relationships is adjusting to shifts and changes in yourself and your loved ones. This can sometimes mean saying goodbye.

You have to let go of people you love when they die. You have to let go when a romantic relationship ends. Sometimes it's adjusting to the end of a chapter in a relationship — when your child moves out of the house to go to college, for instance. Some of these goodbyes involve speaking your truth to another person and some involve only speaking your truth to yourself and holding yourself with integrity through your grief and sadness.

One of the hardest moments in my life was telling my son that his dad was moving out of the house and we were getting divorced. My entire body hurt. I felt like I was going to throw up and like a thousand-pound monster was sitting on my chest. In that initial conversation, I held him while he cried. I told him I loved him so much, that there is nothing he could have done to change the situation and that whatever he was feeling about it was normal and ok. And we all survived. I stayed in my integrity, I spoke my truth, and I held space for him to have his own feelings and reactions. Still, five years later, my son will occasionally say to me, "I wish you and Daddy still lived in the same house." Every time he says that it feels like a sword is slicing through my chest. I can't do anything to fix the pain and sadness he feels about it, no matter how much I wish I could. All I can do is love him through it and model integrity in my own authenticity and vulnerability.

Sometimes he says, "I wish I could spend more time with Daddy. You know I love you, Mom, but I miss Daddy a lot."

In these moments, a part of me wants to scream out, "It's not my fault!! Blame your daddy for ... [fill in the blank]!" Another part of me feels hurt by his words and wants to hurt him back and say, "Fine! Just go live with him, then! See how you like it after a few weeks without me!"

Thankfully I have my tools and enough practice of holding myself through pain to not allow those parts of me to react. I remember that Oliver has a right to miss his dad. It would be weird if he didn't. With practice I remember that it's incredibly important for me to show him that he can trust me with his feelings at twelve years old. I am building a foundation of love, safety, and acceptance in our relationship now, so that as he gets older and his feelings and experiences get more complex and challenging, he knows he can trust me and come to me for support and comfort.

I have also experienced the difficult situation of speaking my truth, knowing the person would be hurt, when I managed a soup kitchen. I had to fire employees for the first time in my life; it was terrifying. I learned so much about myself and human nature through those experiences, though. I had one man yell insults and threaten me bodily harm. Another man acted like he didn't care at all and ran out of the office.

One woman I had to fire tried a mind-boggling array of strategies to change my mind — first insulting me, then crying and acting meek, then threatening me. In hindsight, I was able to see clearly how each of these reactions resulted from a strategy that person had developed as a child. Their reactions were not really about me personally; the protector parts of their personality were in charge in those moments. This is important to remember in preparation for having a difficult, truthful conversation with someone in your life. You can remind yourself that their protectors are bound to kick in and they may say or do upsetting things. By reflecting on this ahead of time, you can emotionally prepare yourself so that their reactions don't trigger your own defensive responses in the moment.

I have also been on the receiving end of painful truths. A guy broke up with me, which is always unpleasant, but he explained that he was too "messed up" to be with me. He said he loved me very much, and that's why he had to break it off. He said he needed to "get his shit together on his own" and then we could be together in the future. I did not respond from a centered or grounded place at all. I cried, yelled, insulted, pleaded, and bargained.

Looking back on myself at that time, I definitely feel embarrassment and shame. I couldn't accept the truth that he was telling me — that he just did not want to be with me anymore. The relationship was not working for him. I can give him credit now, though, that he did his best to own his decision. He never insulted me back, was never mean.

When I think of him and the ending of the relationship now, years later, I still feel pain. I still have a voice in my head that says, *Maybe one day? Maybe when I'm 60 he'll call me up and say he's ready to love me now.* I also have other thoughts and feelings that I have developed over the years. I have the knowledge that I am in a happy, joyful relationship now with an amazing man who shows me every day that he loves me. I have gratitude for the experience and growth I gained through that relationship. I learned a ton about caring for myself through pain and rejection and how to pull myself out of despair and sadness because of him. I learned that no amount of love and desire for another person is enough if that person does not choose to love me.

Another difficult and vulnerable situation in close relationships is when you see a loved one suffering in some way and you cannot help them feel better. Is there anything more painful than watching someone you care about suffer, knowing that you have the ability and tools to help them feel better, but also knowing that they cannot accept your help in that moment? For me, it feels like there's a wood chipper in my chest, shredding my heart.

Sometimes the most vulnerable heartbreaking situation is when you have to let go of the belief that you know what anyone else's path in life is. Because I have spent all my life learning about health — through nutrition, exercise, meditation, relationships — this is something that has been a lifelong journey for me. I feel so much more comfortable when I think that I have the solution that will alleviate a loved ones' suffering.

I only recently came to a place of peace with these situations. The first insight that helped me enormously came from my former therapist. She helped me when my sister was diagnosed with breast cancer. If I were diagnosed with cancer, given my beliefs on medicine and healing and resulting from my years of studying biology, natural medicine, nutrition, etc., I would try to heal myself holistically through natural medicines. When I first heard my sister's diagnosis I wanted to fly out to California and take charge of her treatment — force a "healing boot camp" on her. Or at least make her call all the naturopathic doctors I knew and choose that road for herself.

But she didn't. She chose to fight the cancer with chemotherapy and radiation. Her choice triggered a tsunami-strength rush of anger inside me that she was choosing what looked to me like a self-destructive path. I was furious at her, at her doctors, and at the entire American medical system for not supporting a more holistic approach for her. I was furious at myself for not being able to force her into believing and choosing the same as me.

Finally, after a session consisting mostly of me ranting about all of the above, my therapist said, "You are not an all-powerful, all knowing being, Margot. You cannot know what is going to heal her. She may get better from chemo and radiation. She may not. She may have gotten better with natural medicines. She may not have. You just can't know."

Of course, she was correct. It was arrogant of me to think I knew best what my sister needed. But thinking I knew best allowed me to stay in my anger, an emotion I am much more comfortable with than sadness and fear. It was extremely difficult for me to let go of the anger and look at the vulnerability that was hiding underneath it. I had an overwhelming fear of her dying as well as oceans of sadness for her pain and suffering.

Letting go of the sense of personal control in life will feel very vulnerable and frightening at first. It can feel like stepping off a cliff, with your body in free fall. It can feel like standing naked before the world, watching a huge storm bearing down on you. The protector parts of you will put up a darn good fight against letting go — the biggest fight of their existence, possibly.

On the other side of that letting go, though, is the most delicious sense of peace and ease. The peace comes from being in alignment with the deep truth that you can only control yourself — your choices, and nothing else.

The ease comes from the release of the burden of having to control everything around you. The peace also comes from recognizing that it's not your job in this life to understand, much less direct or control, anyone else's path. Their path is between them and God or the Universe or Mother Nature. You can't know that either, frankly. Your path is to understand your life, your mission, your purpose in this life. Even if that path turns out to be helping, teaching, coaching, or guiding other people, the same truth applies. You may be the wisest, most knowledgeable human on the planet, but your only choice is still to walk your own path. Dictating another person's path is a distraction from your purpose.

Your path to healthy, joyful relationships has taken you through some difficult, challenging moments. You learned a new way to acknowledge, understand, and react to emotional pain. You discovered the delicious peace and freedom that results from courageously facing out-of-integrity moments in your life, then both took responsibility and forgave yourself for them. You were able to step more fully into vulnerability with yourself and your loved ones — in recognition that only through authentic vulnerability can you build rock-solid, honest, loving relationships. Congratulations — you made it through the hardest parts. Onwards towards expanding the fun, joy, and pleasure in your day-to-day life and within all your close relationships!

PART THREE

PURSUE PLEASURE, CHOOSE LOVE

In this part I ask you to commit to seeking more fun in your life and expanding your capacity for pleasure. As you know both from your own experience and from our discussions here, nobody gets through life without episodes of pain, and those painful moments are always an opportunity for you to deepen your loving compassionate relationship with yourself. I am not advocating for seeking out pain or constantly focusing your attention on the negative: you can always do your best to avoid pain when possible. But attempting to eliminate all pain from your life is futile, as we've also seen — unless you are choosing not to have any meaningful relationships. As Wesley, the sort-of hero in one of my favorite movies, *The Princess Bride*, says, "Life is pain ... Anyone who tells you different is selling something."

You know pain is in your past and will inevitably be in your future, which is precisely why I advocate choosing to stuff as much fun, joy, and pleasure as you can into every moment of your life. I want you to commit to seeking joy and fun as often as possible in your life and expanding your capacity for pleasure. Think of a flower always turning to face the sun. Orient yourself toward pleasure: seek it out and build up your capacity to recognize pleasure in many different situations and unexpected circumstances.

Are you starting to ask yourself, *How does this relate to having healthy, close relationships?* Or, *How woo woo is this woman, thinking I can just choose to feel pleasure at any time?!*

Trust me, I have spent more than enough time in the "woo woo" world of yoga and meditation attempting to convince myself that I could simply choose to "just be happy." I know now, however, that without necessary tools, without doing the hard work to love all of yourself, without taking the journey into your own deep dark bits, many of you will never experience the happiness and joyful relationships that you are seeking. Since you have been doing that deeper work and are practicing with the self-building tools I am sharing here, you are ready to explore and expand your relationship with pleasure and joy — Yay!!

To explain what I mean about exploring and expanding your relationship with pleasure, I would like to share a story about a dear friend of mine, Arabella — one of my first mentors in my journey toward self acceptance, trust, and love.

I met Arabella when she volunteered at an event I was hosting, producing, and cooking for, a pop up, pay-what-you-can brunch at the local community center. She's a curvy woman in her 60s with mischievous blue eyes and long, flowy, dyed-red hair. Something about her intrigued me enormously and we made plans to spend time together socially. A few weeks later, I found myself at her kitchen table gabbing away while delighting in the delicious vegetarian meal she had prepared. After dinner I popped up and headed to the sink to do the dishes, following the unwritten social rule "If one person cooks, the other cleans up." I felt happy to clean up, especially because, being a professional chef, people rarely cook for me!

But Arabella stopped me. "I can do the dishes any day," she said. "Time with Margot is special. Let's leave them for now."

Whoa! My mind was blown. Arabella chose pleasure over chores, "shoulds," and "supposed to's" without guilt or shame. She made choosing pleasure seem like not just an acceptable choice but the most logical one. I had never experienced anything like that before and my brain flashed the words, *Does not compute! Does not compute!*

14

PERMISSION TO FEEL PLEASURE

Arabella short-circuited my brain again a few weeks later. Snow was falling outside; I was feeling lazy and I posted something whiney on Facebook bemoaning my situation. She commented in response, "What if it were pleasurable?"

What?! What did she possibly mean by that? She doesn't know how stressful my job is! How hard I work! How irritating *x, y, z* people are! What does she know?! Pleasure is *impossible* at my job!

Despite the immediate resistance her comment triggered, those five words wiggled into my brain. Without consciously choosing to, I found myself having way more fun than usual at work that day. I laughed at things that in the past would have irritated me tremendously. I discovered that it was easy to not take people's negative attitudes personally. It was as if I was ensconced within a golden shimmery bubble that protected me and allowed me to have a pleasure-filled day!

It seems that all I had needed was permission to enjoy myself and a little gentle nudge in that direction. And if that's all you need, then here it is: I give you permission, along with a gentle little nudge, to seek out pleasure today.

However, you may be experiencing strong resistance at this point, just like I did. A voice in your head may be saying, *Margot is clearly out to lunch. Life is hard. If I traipse around like some hippie-dippie flower child, acting like life is all rainbows and giggles, I will look ridiculous, not get anything accomplished and wind up homeless and jobless, begging for change, and be in for a rude surprise when life inevitably throws some crap my way.*

Fair enough, but let me offer three counter-beliefs that I believe hold more truth:

1. **You always risk looking ridiculous.** To some people having fun at work may look ridiculous. It's very possible that those people are themselves scared of having fun or have forgotten how. To other folks you may look ridiculous when you mope around feeling sorry for yourself when you have so much to be thankful for. Also, your fun and joy may look very different from other peoples'. There may be no rainbows or flowers in sight. Your pleasure on a particular day may be spending three hours alone cleaning your house or working on your car. Find out what brings you joy, fun, and pleasure and seek that out. No matter what you are doing, you run the risk of looking ridiculous to someone, so it's pointless to let that keep you from doing anything.

2. **You can get more done if you find the fun in doing it.** I am not suggesting that you "shirk your duties," stop going to work, or let a week's worth of dishes pile up in your sink. I am suggesting that by using your natural creativity you can find more fun in situations that you normally would automatically label "awful" or "boring." When you approach situations with this attitude you might find you actually accomplish more in a day — partly because you will not waste time stalling and procrastinating before getting to the thing

you dread and partly because you will feel energized afterwards, instead of needing to decompress or spend time complaining about how awful it was.

One of my favorite recent examples of this in my own life was when I realized that I dread going to my yearly gynecologist appointments. As usual, I found myself sitting in the stupid paper gown, staring at the ugly ceiling, getting more and more angry and frustrated by being kept waiting for so long for the doctor to make her cursory 10-minute visit to my nether regions. Later at home I was struck suddenly with a simple thought: Why was I upset about spending time by myself in a quiet room with nothing to do? This is something that I choose to do almost every day; I call it meditating. Could it really be that the only reason I had felt angry and frustrated was because of my perception of that situation? Because I had expected to not have to sit there as long as I did? So, what if next time I had a doctor appointment, I planned differently? What if I changed how I thought about the visit and labeled it "me time." I could bring my iPod to listen to music or a book I've been wanting to read for years. I could plan to use that time to meditate or journal or even write a letter to my body, telling her how much I appreciate all she does for me by keeping me healthy, moving, breathing, digesting food, etc., every day for the past 42 years. The possibilities are almost endless; all it needed was a shift in perspective. And as I mentioned I actually would be more productive that day than if I were to sit in the waiting room, fuming, and stewing in my anger.

3. **Give yourself permission to seek out fun and pleasure.** As I've already argued, life *will* throw crap at you. You know that already; no surprise there. Doesn't it therefore make even more sense to seek out pleasure

and fun whenever and however you can? Why choose to feel crappy when you can choose to feel pleasure, peace, or joy?

When you allow yourself to feel, deep in your bones, that you deserve joy and that you are worthy of pleasure, you are shoring up your foundation of safety and love. This allows you to be able to weather life's storms a little more easily rather than drown in them. You know that there will be days, weeks, months, even, when you will feel tossed around by rough waves of sadness and grief, but you can more easily remember that pleasure and joy always come back into your life as well.

15

THE POSSIBILITY OF PLEASURE

Thus, I invite you to begin your "pleasure-seeking practice." Starting is simple but not necessarily easy. You begin by asking yourself, "How could this be pleasurable?" at various points throughout your normal day: in traffic, waiting at a doctor's office, doing mindless paperwork at your job, changing a diaper. Eventually begin to challenge yourself to see how far you can go — what is the part of your life you dread the most and can you bring some fun and lightness to it?

For most of us, this is a lifelong practice that we never fully master. It gets easier with time, but you may need reminders. For some reason our human brains quickly latch onto pain and suffering rather than joy and pleasure. But we can create new neural pathways over time with focus and practice.

Children can be incredibly helpful and supportive in this arena, reminding you to look for the fun and joy in a moment. Just the other day I had to get some work done on my car and I took my kids with me to the auto shop. It was a simple job and I hoped the wait would be short, but it started to drag on and I started to feel annoyed and frustrated. A TV was on in the waiting room so my kids were watching it with the typical, glazed over, "boob tube" expressions.

Luckily, in that moment I remembered the practice of asking myself, "How can this be more pleasurable?" The answer came to mind immediately. We could just walk home from the auto shop. I had groceries with me, but it wasn't a super long walk and the weather was cool and clear, so off we went. We wound up having such a good time: both my kids talked my ear off the whole way home, which has become sort of unusual at their age. I was reminded of how kids will often open up more easily when engaging in a physical activity with a parent and also when next to a parent instead of face to face.

Thich Nhat Hanh, a renowned Buddhist monk and teacher has taught me a lot about how to seek pleasure. He was speaking with Krista Tippett on her radio program "On Being" about how doing dishes can be a very pleasant sensual experience. The hot water on your hands, the slippery soap feeling, the satisfaction of making things clean. He explained that it's the anticipation of the chore that can make it feel unpleasant as well as the stories we attach to the act itself.

Unbelievably, I was actually standing at the sink doing dishes when this came on the radio. At that time, I was spending an enormous amount of time doing dishes every day because I was working as a private chef (lots of dishes) and was a single mom of two kids with a broken dishwasher (lots and *lots* of dishes.) I was not experiencing anything remotely resembling a pleasurable sensual experience. Instead I was thinking, *I shouldn't have to do this! I wish I had more money to buy a dishwasher. I'm a failure for my failed marriage and now I have to do all this work by myself!*

Thich Nhat Hanh's insight made me stop and pay attention to my thoughts in that moment. I realized what heavy feelings of failure, sadness, and hopelessness I had attached to this particular chore. My mind had created a story that equated washing dishes with my insecurities about failing at marriage and as a chef. This caused a cascade of uncomfortable emotions every time I had to do dishes. There were many nights when I would cry into the sink after I put my kids to bed. And even more nights when I would slam the dishes around, taking my anger, frustration, and disappointment at myself and my ex-husband out on the unwitting cutlery.

Once I was able to see the stories I had created and attached to the simple act of washing dishes, I was able to let go of them and open myself to the pleasure available there. I could put music on and shimmy around in front of my sink, singing horribly, with nobody around to groan in pain.

So, I challenge you to open yourself to the possibility of pleasure. Ask yourself, "How can I look for fun, pleasure, and joy this week, even in the most unlikely of places? What meanings have I been attaching to simple acts that have caused them to feel dreaded and painful? What do *you* need to do to feel worthy and deserving of more joy, fun, and pleasure in my daily routine? Remember, if I can find fun in doing dishes, you too can discover pleasure in unlikely places.

16

PLEASURE AND GRATITUDE

The surest and quickest way that I have found to increase my moments of pleasure and joy throughout my daily life is with a regular "gratitude practice." You can start very simply by saying to yourself: *I am grateful to be alive. I am grateful for my lungs for breathing. I am grateful for my bed. I am grateful for clean water to drink.* The more you practice gratitude, the happier you will feel. The more you practice gratitude, the more you will notice how much you have to be grateful for. The more you focus on feeling gratitude for the people you love, the more love you will feel for them. The more gratitude you show your loved ones, the more love, affection, and appreciation they will show you. The more time you focus on what you have to feel grateful for, the more love you will be able to give and receive every day. Committing yourself to a regular — daily, if possible — gratitude practice is the surest path to having healthy, joyful, sustainable relationships. Write it down, tell it to God before bed, speak it around the dinner table, meditate on it. There are myriad ways to practice gratitude. Just do it.

17

YOUR PLEASURE TREASURE CHEST

I call your internal capacity to store and access pleasure your "pleasure treasure chest," and keeping it full is helpful in building healthy, joyful relationships with loved ones. Having your own pleasure treasure chest to pull from helps you stay centered and avoid enmeshment situations in romantic relationships. It is so common for people who are falling in love or have recently found a new romantic partner to start believing that their happiness and joy in life depends on that partner. We will discuss this in more detail in a later chapter but for the purpose of this argument, I believe it is sufficient to remind you that *you are a sovereign being.* You are responsible for your emotions, your actions, and reactions. You can get triggered by another human of course — other humans trigger emotions in us all day every day — but they are still your feelings. You can choose to be around people who trigger pleasurable feelings in you more often than painful feelings, but the truth is that all the feelings of love and appreciation you feel at any moment are being generated by you. When you embrace this truth and keep a full treasure chest, you become more resilient to rejection or disappointment, you become less reactive to other people's bad behaviors, and you have a reserve from which to act with integrity.

Focusing on your own treasure chest also helps you avoid going down the rabbit hole of putting another person's feelings and needs before your own. This is such a common dynamic with parents in our culture currently, and one in which I spent quite a few years of my life mucking around in myself. Moms and dads experience the pressure to sacrifice themselves for their children in different ways, but both sexes suffer under an overwhelming conditioning in our culture of how to be "good parents." Often, men feel pressure to take on the entire burden of financial responsibility during the early months of their child's life (this is generalizing, of course, but there is truth here). For many women, especially first-time mothers, there is incredible fear of doing something wrong with our babies. When my son was first born, I was so overwhelmed with fear that I was doing everything wrong that thinking about what made me feel good wasn't even on the radar. I didn't consciously choose to put his needs first at the expense of my own, but he screamed to get his needs met so much more loudly than I could have at the time!

I also recommend focusing on your pleasure treasure chest to understand very clearly what makes you feel good in order to share that information with people in your life. The people that love you want to do things to make you happy, right? Have you ever known someone whom it was impossible to buy presents for or do nice things for? I have, and I did not enjoy it. It brings me pleasure to do nice things for people I care about and when someone denies me that pleasure, I do not appreciate it.

It is also helpful to know what brings you pleasure so that you can find people who find fun and pleasure in similar things to you. They don't have to have the exact same list, which would be impossible anyway, but you will want some of the same things because many of the things that bring you pleasure are even more fun when shared with someone you care about.

Now that you understand the need for having a personal pleasure treasure chest, how do you go about filling it? I remind you to be patient with yourself. Building up your capacity for pleasure is accomplished step by step, with practice and focus. Remember that you need to be responsible for your own feelings, the pleasurable and painful, in order to build and enjoy healthy, joyful relationships.

In addition to consciously building your pleasure treasure chest, I wholeheartedly encourage you to commit to doing some kind of regular self-love meditation. Every day is fantastic. Three times per week is great as well. If you have your own practices that you already love, wonderful! Self-love practices are necessary throughout all times in your life but will be especially crucial now as you embark out of the muddy, sticky ruts of old relationship patterning.

I learned an important lesson in self-love a few years ago when I signed up for Layla Martin's Jade Egg course.[8] At the time, I believed my main goal was to solve the occasional incontinence problem I had since giving birth to my first baby; the fact that a regular Jade Egg practice increases sexual pleasure was an added bonus. The homework in the introductory module of the course is a self breast massage: which can increase self-love enormously. Well, I wasn't having it. *I don't need to do that*, I thought. *Get me to the actual Jade Egg stuff.* So, I skipped that part.

About a year later, when I had signed up for Layla's Sex, Love and Relationship Coaching program a bunch of my

---

[8] See www.laylamartin.com. Originally the jade egg practice was implemented for improving physical and spiritual health, mainly by bringing more power to the chi muscle to enhance the chi or life force and bring the sexual energy inward and upward where it could be transformed into higher energy.

fellow students decided to go through the Jade Egg program together, and I was faced with the breast massage practice again. This time my "good student" subpersonality took the reins and pushed through my resistance.

I put on the self breast massage audio, got myself ready with massage oil and a cozy blanket and began. Immediately the tears started coursing down my cheeks. In that moment I realized that I had never in my life touched myself with the pure simple intention of loving myself; showing myself affection and tenderness. I cried for all the years that I had, at best, been tolerant towards myself and at worst been judgmental, critical, or just plain mean. I cried in gratitude for Layla's wisdom and willingness to share her gifts with me and I cried in gratitude for finally being ready to receive her gifts and do the simple practice. I cried for myself as a young girl, hating my breasts, standing in front of the mirror, hating so many things about my perfect, beautiful body. And I cried in recognition of the ease and comfort I was creating in myself with such a simple exercise.

Remember that you are almost guaranteed to feel resistance when you choose to begin any sort of self love meditation or practice, just as I did with the breast massage. You may forget to do it or convince yourself something else needs doing or, if you're like me, that you know what's best.

This is why you need support when changing old patterns of behavior, thoughts, or feelings. Ask for support from friends and loved ones. Hire a coach. Do not fall into the trap of thinking, *I don't need anyone. I am a strong warrior — I can do it all!* When I start to listen to my internal voices telling me that I do not need help from anyone, I remind myself of my experience giving birth to my son Oliver. I was in labor for 42 hours. By the time he was ready to come out and my midwife told me to push, I was beyond exhausted and completely petrified. I didn't think I could do it. But my midwife looked me in the eye and said, "You can do this. I believe in you."

The journey was mine alone: I had to do the work of birthing my baby. But I needed to know that someone else believed in me. She couldn't do the work for me, but she could support and encourage me on my journey.

Humans are tribal animals. Whatever your journey is and wherever it takes you, you need support from other people to get there. In order to support you in this way, I have created a Facebook group here - http://bit.ly/ChooseLovetheBook in which you can connect with people going through their own journeys. You can also find links to all the practices suggested here - https://margotschulman.vipmembervault.com.

18

GIVE & RECEIVE LOVE

The last step that I ask you to commit to in order to create healthy, loving, sustainable relationships in all areas of your life may seem simplistic at first glance. You need to choose to give and show love to your people, and you have to choose to receive the love that they give you. This seems simple, but perhaps because of that it can be so easily forgotten.

Before we dive into figuring out how to give and receive love I want to take some time to gain some necessary clarity on the term *love* itself. What is love, actually? Is it a noun or a verb or both somehow? Can you choose to feel it or is it something that happens to you — that you fall into, like an unseen hole in the ground?

We spend so much time talking about love in our culture: falling in and out of love, hoping someone loves us, wondering if they love us enough. Popular music, film, and books are predominantly about love and relationships. Even in the area of career, people talk about "doing what you love." There are so many different definitions floating around in our culture these days, as well. People talk about love as a verb. We often throw the word around willy-nilly: "I love my kids," and also "I love chocolate peanut butter ice cream." How can we possibly use the same word to describe the complexity of our feelings towards our children with the simple physical sensation we experience when consuming ice cream?

We make it such a big deal to say "I love you" to a new lover or partner. But how do we know that the other person even defines this the same way that we do? How many couples actually take the time to discuss what love means to them? Have you ever asked someone you are dating how they define love?

And what does it mean to say, "I love you, but I am not in love with you?" Have you heard that one before?

I remember learning that the Inuit language has over 50 words for snow (if you ask a linguist they may debate this, but that's beside the point here). I remember thinking, *Fifty words for* snow *and we only have one word for* love?! *That is ridiculous.*

I can think of at least 10 distinct categories that need to have their own word in my vocabulary, and that is excluding love I have for particular foods, smells, and all sorts of natural beauty like the ocean, certain trees, etc.:

1. Love for my children
2. Love for my parents
3. Love for my sister
4. Love for my closest friends
5. Love for old friends that I have grown apart from
6. Love for people whose company I really enjoy but hardly ever spend time with
7. Love for my pets
8. Love for my boyfriend
9. Love for all the teachers I have ever had
10. Love of myself

I could go on and on.

The common thread I have found most useful when discussing love as a noun is that it is a complex stew of emotions which creates particular sensations of warmth in your chest, along with a physical urge to move towards the object of the love. The heat is often accompanied by sensations of throbbing, tingling, tightness, or expansion, and can extend up and out into your throat, arms, and face and even down into your belly. Another useful common thread is that love is the emotion that triggers particular thought patterns such as, "I feel so grateful she is in my life," "I want to protect him," "I want to be near her all the time," "What an incredible person he is," and "I hope she cares for me, too."

Let's take a minute to sit with these ideas. How do you feel about this definition of love? What thoughts come up for you as you read this? Does this definition feel complete or are you thinking that it's too simplistic? As I ponder these questions for myself, there is still a part of me that thinks love cannot be as simple as just physical sensations and particular thoughts. It often feels so complicated, right? But I will hold fast to this definition along with the caveat that love often feels complicated because of all the meanings, expectations, and other emotions we attach to our love.

Before I unpack that, let's try a simple exercise you can do right now to reflect on whether or how you love particular people in your life. Just close your eyes and picture the person standing in front of you, a few feet away, looking at you and holding their arms out as if offering an embrace. Notice how your body reacts. Do you feel the urge to move towards them for a hug or to turn away? Do you feel "lit up" inside or scared and nervous? Does your face automatically begin to smile?

Now for some people you love, the above exercise may be complicated. For instance, if you close your eyes and picture your mother standing in front of you, you may not feel lit up inside. You may have a strained relationship with her or be in the middle of an argument when reading these words. That's okay and normal. Stay with the meditation and pay attention to your body's signals. What do you feel in your heart and chest? What signals are your protectors sending?

I have already explained that my relationship with my sister is quite complicated. When I close my eyes and picture her standing in front of me, with her arms open for a hug, I feel an immediate rush of heat in my chest, my face gets hot, and I feel tears welling up in my eyes. I hear the thoughts in my head saying, *I can't believe she's offering me a hug. I'm so happy. I feel so grateful.*

This shows me that my love for her is real and, deep down, still quite simple. Our relationship feels complicated because of all the history we've accumulated over our lives together: moments of connection and joy as well as misunderstandings, disappointments and pain. I have so many different feelings about my sister, which can feel confusing and heavy, but the love itself feels uncomplicated and light.

It is helpful to have this simple yet solid foundation of love to build upon as we dive deeper into the inquiry around defining love as a *verb*. If we accept the previous definition of love the noun as a set of physical sensations and thoughts that arise without your control, then how is it possible to choose to love people? Why do we care so much if other people love us or not? How can we give and receive love?

I would argue that you cannot control what or whom you love. You cannot turn your love on or off because you cannot control your body's and mind's reactions in a moment.

Consider the simple example of my first "love," chocolate peanut butter ice cream. This relationship began when I was 16 years old and working my first job at a Baskin Robbins ice cream shop. It was love at first bite. Chocolate peanut butter ice cream was there for me when I was nervous that I would mess up someone's order (it was my first job, remember). It was there to help me celebrate when the boy I liked came into the shop and asked me out. Chocolate peanut butter ice cream was there, by my side, through good times and bad, and it always made me feel good. Seems like a pretty healthy relationship right?

Did I choose to love chocolate peanut butter ice cream at 16 years old? No.

Do I choose to love it now, 26 years later? No.

My body still reacts to the flavors and the texture of the ice cream in a way that I have no control over. When I put a spoonful of chocolate peanut butter ice cream in my mouth, my tongue responds to the sweetness and creamy texture. The pleasure centers in my brain light up from the sugar and chocolate. Bittersweet nostalgic memories come up too — I am 16 years old again, in all my confused, hormonal, dramatic glory.

I cannot choose *the feeling of love* that arises when looking at a tub of chocolate peanut butter ice cream behind the glass. I can, however, choose *how to react to that love*: I can choose what kind of relationship I desire to have with the ice cream. When I bring my kids to the ice cream shop, I allow myself to feel all the feelings and hear all the thoughts in my head. I allow myself to feel the nostalgia and even remember the taste sensations in my mouth. I remember that I can choose to order and eat some or not. I remind myself that I do not enjoy the feeling of stomach cramps and gassiness that I get after eating ice cream. I feel the love for the ice cream, I find pleasure in the memory of its taste, I feel grateful that I have the willpower to not eat any and joy that I have been able to create a relationship with this food that makes me feel really good!

The same does apply to relationships with people. A few years ago, I met a man I will call Frank. It was "love at first sight" for me. I felt like I had known him for years. All the physical sensations associated with love were there: warmth in my chest, tingling in my arms and belly. The thoughts of love were there as well: "I like everything about him!" and "I want to be near him all the time!"

So how did I react and respond at the time? Well, I fell for him hard. I decided that we were soul mates and about to embark on the most amazing love adventure the world had ever seen. I felt that the universe and God had aligned specifically to bring us together to love each other.

And all that may be true. I cannot truly know the behind-the-scenes plans of God and the Universe. But I did learn other important truths about that situation. I learned that being in a relationship with Frank was extremely unhealthy for me at that time in my life. Why? Many, many reasons including that we needed and wanted very different things in a romantic relationship. He believed deeply in "free love" or polyamory and, while I understood and appreciated those ideas intellectually, in practice they did not feel good to me at all. He also had never done his own healing work around sexual and emotional abuse he suffered as a child and was not open to doing any of that work at the time.

So, I loved him and I let him go. It was not easy. I grieved for the end of the relationship. I grieved for the death of the fantasy of our future together. Even now, as I write about it, I feel a tightness in my chest and a burning in my throat. I hear a kind of whiny voice inside my head saying, *Maybe it could still work!* and *Remember how good you felt when you were with him?!*

Now, when his face pops up in my Facebook feed and I allow myself to feel love for him, it feels sort of bittersweet in my body. Part of me still longs to be near him and that's okay. If I try to push that feeling away it only gets stronger. I allow myself to just sit with my longing for him. I breathe and remember that it's just one part of what's happening inside me at the moment. I am still breathing. I can feel my body on the couch. I can even imagine sending him love through the universe. I can feel love and longing for him and choose to not call him.

19

CONTROL AND RELEASE

One of the most important steps to heal from unhealthy relationships and break out of old patterns is to get really clear on what parts of the process you can control and what you cannot. Once you figure that out, you can focus on letting go of any internal judgment and criticism you are placing on yourself or others for the parts over those things you cannot control.

What does this mean?

Let's return to the example of chocolate peanut butter ice cream. In the past, I have at times judged myself harshly for not being able to "get over" a desire to eat it. I would hear stories in my head along the lines of, *You are so weak. You have no self-control. What's wrong with you? Why can't you be one of those women who walks right on by the ice cream case without a moment's hesitation?* These thoughts would then lead to feeling sorry for myself or guilty, which would then lead me to give up on the idea of ever being able to change my patterns since I was clearly a messed-up failure.

In the case of my relationship with Frank, thinking about him would cause me to spiral downwards into a well of self-beratement way deeper than the ice cream judgment. My head would fill with thoughts along the lines of, *You are such a fool! Falling for another alcoholic. What's wrong with you that you still pine for him, after how he treated you?! You deserve to be alone because you keep failing in relationships.*

Thankfully, I now have the tools to stop myself before I go very deep into that well of self-recrimination and judgment. I use my tools to come back to my deep knowing that I am always doing my best. I am learning and growing and failing and getting up again to learn and grow and fail some more. I know that I cannot choose how my body reacts to people any more than I can control how it reacts to ice cream. I don't have to get down on myself for feeling uncontrollable sensations in response to certain people and particular situations.

What's wonderfully freeing about releasing what I cannot control is that it gives me the space in a particular moment, when I feel a longing for someone or something, to make a different choice about what action to take in response to those feelings. When I forget my tools and wind up spiraling down into negative criticism, there is no space for me to pause and act from my grounded center.

Next time you start judging yourself harshly for feeling a particular desire for someone or something, try letting yourself off the hook. See how it feels. Ask yourself, "What if my best friend was having this experience and telling me about it? Would I berate her/him for their feelings? Or would I feel compassion and offer them support and love and perhaps a reminder that they are doing the best they can and that you believe in their success?"

Along with learning to let go of self-criticism, the other crucial part of this process is learning to avoid the common pitfall of labeling the object of your desire or love "bad." This type of judgment is a choice we all have made at certain times in our lives. It's a protection mechanism: if the thing or person we can't have is bad, we feel less sad about the loss. Sometimes labeling the desired person or object bad allows us to feel anger, too, which for many of us is a much more comfortable emotion than sadness: *Ice cream is evil! The terrible sugar companies created it to turn us all into sugar addicts and make us slaves to their evil products!* (Don't laugh, I have actually said things like this at times in my life.)

How many times have you decided a person you loved was bad or crazy when the relationship ended? This is the same person that up until very recently you had felt incredible affection and compassion for. It's reasonable to assume that the person who just broke up with you is not evil because of your love for them. If you suspect that someone in your life does have serious mental health and/or substance abuse issues, you need extra time, focus, and support to rebuild your self-trust, look back through the relationship for red flags and heal from any trauma or abuse you experiences.

In the case of healing from the end of a relationship with a relatively mentally stable person there are a few additional problems with labeling them as bad, evil, or crazy beyond the question of whether it's actually truth or fiction. One problem is that it keeps you in a loop of self judgment: if ice cream or your ex-girlfriend is evil, then what does that mean about you that you still want them, miss them, feel love for them? It would have to mean that there is something wrong with you too, that you are stupid or broken for failing to see the evil earlier or for continuing to desire it. Or it could mean that you were a poor victim who fell prey to the powerful wiles of an evil substance or person. If you go down this second path it sets you up to feel powerless, terrified that you will fall prey again to future evil. Neither direction sets you onto a path of creating healthy, joyful, relationships in your future.

Try for a moment to imagine that these objects of your love are neutral — not angels from heaven and not spawn of the devil. Ice cream can be both delicious *and* lead to stomach cramps. Former lovers have good *and* bad qualities. Sometimes they act in ways that make you feel good *and* sometimes they act in ways that make you feel bad. They are human, as are you. The more you can let go of labels and judgments, the more freedom you create in yourself to make choices based from a place of clarity, self-trust, and inner wisdom.

When you are able to let go of judgment about yourself and others, you also create space inside yourself to feel more gratitude for the pleasure, joy, and goodness you have in your life every day. I love the quote from Dr. Seuss, "Don't cry because it's over, smile because it happened."

Of course, this is easier said than done. It takes commitment, practice, and time. You cannot choose the sensations or thoughts that occur from moment to moment. That's the bad news. The good news is that you can choose how to react and respond to those sensations and thoughts in the moment. In addition, you can consciously, with practice, over time, build up new thought patterns and physical sensations to shift those old patterns and create more and more acceptance and compassion within yourself.

So, even if you cannot really choose to love, since love is a set of physical sensations and thought patterns that arise spontaneously, you still can choose how you deal with those feelings and thoughts and what actions you take with the people around you in response to those thoughts and sensations. You can choose how to be in relationship with the objects of your love. You can choose how you love them. I love chocolate peanut butter ice cream, even if I never eat another spoonful in my life. That might be the best relationship for me to have with that object: loving it from across the glass case at the ice cream shop.

It is up to you to figure out how to make every relationship in your life the healthiest, most supportive, and most joyful for you. It is up to you to figure out what your needs and desires are in that relationship and communicate them clearly to the other person. Sounds simple, right? If only! But this is the work that is necessary to have healthy, joyful relationships in all areas of your life. And it will look different for every relationship you have.

20

SET YOUR EXPECTATIONS

One thing that will be helpful in every close relationship you have in your life is to shift your expectations about what you will feel and experience because of that relationship. You will save yourself a ton of regret, anger, judgment, and hurt if you enter into all relationships knowing that there will be moments of pain along the way. One huge and simple way to prevent unnecessary suffering is to remember what choosing to love someone deeply entails. Relationships will cause you moments of pain, but is the alternative preferable? If you numb yourself to pain then you numb yourself to joy, excitement, love, and connection, as well.

I agree with the Buddhist teachings that attachments are what cause pain and suffering; I just disagree that because of this we should strive for non-attachment in all areas of our lives. If I became completely enlightened, in the Buddhist sense, I imagine I would be a terrible mom. My kids need me to be present and attached to them — caring about them in very specific, connected ways (the literature of parenting literally calls it "attachment parenting"). I need to care enough about them and their futures to teach and guide them to become good people. Obviously, I do not know how it feels to be an enlightened soul, but I do know what it feels like to

SET YOUR EXPECTATIONS

be a mother to two amazing children. I would choose that attachment a million times over. I also know what it feels like to be so connected with a lover that we feel connected not only to each other but to all the stars in the universe. I would choose that feeling a million times over.

I choose attachment because to me, the pain is worth it. I cannot choose to be a nun. I choose close loving relationships. But I choose them consciously, knowing that with that choice, I am also choosing the possibility of pain.

I also know that the pain that can come in close loving relationships can be my best teacher; it shows me the places inside myself that need more attention, compassion, and healing. Emotional pain, just like physical pain from a cut or bruise, is always a signal from part of yourself that healing needs to happen there. It is always an opportunity for you to go inward, love yourself more, uncover more of your truth, and create greater integration and understanding within yourself and/or with your loved one.

There will be all kinds of pain, too. Pain is not always the big dramatic kind of someone leaving you (either by choice of by dying). There is the sometimes overlooked pain we experience in our daily lives when your words or actions are misunderstood or your gestures of love go unnoticed and unappreciated. There is the pain of your partner asking you to talk about feelings when you arrive home exhausted after a long day at work. But these are the moments you sign up for when you decide to be in partnership with another human.

There is the pain when your child, the best kid in the universe, tells you that the girl he asked to be his valentine said no. Or the pain of having to say to your daughter, "I have no freaking idea how to help you with this new math." But that's what you sign up for when you decide to become a parent.

When you begin to consciously choose close relationships with full awareness that there will be moments of pain alongside all of the joy and sweetness, something really incredible and surprising begins to happen. Somehow you can begin to actually feel *less pain* during experiences that would have previously felt very painful.

Let's take the relatively trivial example of me trying to learn the "new math" so I can help my daughter figure out her homework. It wasn't going well. There were illustrations and instructions that I didn't understand; none of it was familiar to me. My mind was saying, *This is a waste of my time. You're not going to be able to figure this out.* This thought in turn caused me to feel frustrated and irritated. I heard: *I must be stupid for not understanding 6th grade math,* or *My daughter must think I am stupid for not understanding.* It was just math, but because of the story I told myself I began to feel shame, which can be the most painful emotion of all.

How does this experience change when I remember my commitment to anticipating pain in my role as mother? What if I took a moment and thought to myself, *I chose these kinds of moments, when I chose to have kids.* When I think that, I start feeling gratitude and humility. This allows space for other stories to fill my brain such as, *I am so grateful that my child trusts me to help her with this,* and *I will feel proud of myself when I understand it,* and maybe even *Isadora will feel so proud of herself when she helps me understand the math and that will be very helpful for her.*

Although the above example doesn't have especially heavy emotion attached to it (or maybe you think it has too much!), the concept applies across the board. Let's look at how this can work with a more emotionally charged story: my recent experience of grieving after my aunt died. She was a very special person to me and to everyone who knew her. She always made the people around her feel welcome, loved, appreciated, and special. I will miss her for the rest of my life; her absence at family gatherings will always cause pain. At her memorial, her son (my cousin) shared the story of how his mother would have died giving birth to him were it not for luck and amazing doctors. He felt so clearly how the grief he was experiencing after her death was worth every day he had gotten to have with her in his life before that.

Would any of us choose not to love the people we love if we knew ahead of time that they would leave us at some point? Like it or not, all relationships end. We are mortal creatures and the only things we can count on in this life are change and death. But can you even imagine yourself being you if not for the relationships you had with those people?

The good news is that when you stop trying to hide from suffering, you shift your relationship to it. With practice, you can begin to see the source of your pain and understand that it usually comes from the stories that you create about the situation. Then you can consciously change those stories, writing new ones that will build more pleasant sensations and feelings.

21

COMMIT TO THE PRACTICE

Changing the stories can become a practice for you. Start with the lighter stuff and with time, focus, and practice, you can start to shift the stories, the sensations of heavier emotions, and the meanings of situations. But you have to commit to the practice; it has to be an intentional choice just like every other skill we've discussed in this book.

Committing to choose love, to investing in close relationships, with the full awareness that at some point you will experience pain and loss because of this choice, is brave. As Brené Brown says, in a poster I have hanging on my wall, "Courage is a Heart Word. Love Hard."

Committing to showing your love by caring for and supporting others is another courageous choice. You have to choose to show over and over that you see, hear, and appreciate them for who they are at their core level and are grateful to have them in your life. Committing to choose love goes beyond holding space to filling that space with love, being present and full of kindness and compassion.

Just as important as actively giving love to your people is committing to receiving love and support from them. Your loved ones want to love and support you (If they don't, then you have to let them go). They will not feel happy and fulfilled if their love is blocked, unnoticed, or unappreciated. You have to choose to support your loved ones, build them up more than you tear them down, cheerlead for them more than you criticize. Speak to them with kindness. Show them your affection. Understand their love languages and speak to them in the language they understand. Even in the times and moments when you disagree with a decision they make or feel angry, irritated, or hurt by them, still choose compassion. Choose kindness. Choose thoughtfulness.

Do your best to remember in the hardest moments that you love them.

Remember there is always room for kindness.

This may feel like an easy task in many of your relationships, but what about the hard ones? I know I find it very easy to give and receive love from my children. Even when they anger me or act thoughtlessly, I can remember my love for them within seconds. I feel it in my chest; it is very quickly accessed, at the top of my heart.

With my own parents or my sister, though, it can often be much more challenging to remember compassion, kindness, and thoughtfulness. My love for them can feel harder to access, like it's buried under the weight of many other feelings. Coming back to compassion and kindness with them takes more time and more effort. As Ram Daas once said, "If you think you're enlightened, go spend a week with your family."

It can be very hard in long-term intimate partnerships and marriages, as well. It really takes no effort at all to take your partner for granted, to let resentment over little things or even just boredom and familiarity build up to the point of forgetting to feel, much less show, appreciation and gratitude for the person you chose to commit yourself to. And then of course a lack of appreciation and love by one partner will snowball exponentially in any long-term relationship.

It takes active effort for the entirety of your relationship to resist that smooth slide into boredom, complacency, and resentment. You need incredible patience, vulnerability, and faith to choose to put in that effort and believe that your relationship is worth it.

22

LEARN TO SPEAK LOVE LANGUAGES

One amazing tool that I have found to help in my intimate relationships as well as other long-term relationships — such as those with my parents and sister — is the concept of the five love languages. This is a framework conceived of by the author and former marriage counselor Gary Chapman in his classic book *The 5 Love Languages*. The basic idea is that each of us has one of five particular ways that we recognize love and are able to receive it most easily. Whichever love language makes you feel the most love is also how you generally show love to people. Thus, if you and your partner do not speak the same love language, it may be like speaking two different verbal languages; a lot can be lost in the translation — missed cues, misunderstandings, lack of appreciation.

The five love languages are: Words of Affirmation, Physical Touch, Gifts, Acts of Service and Quality Time. Words of Affirmation are when your partner tells you verbally how much they appreciate, admire, respect, and love you. Physical Touch of course includes physical affection and frequent offers of loving caresses — both sexual and non-sexual. Gifts are pretty straightforward except it is not about the cost of the gift but the meaning behind it. It can be little things like a seashell from a beach that let the loved one know you were thinking of them in a moment when you two were not physically together. Acts of Service is when your loved one does things for you like change the oil in your car without you asking or bake your favorite cookies for you. And Quality Time is simply time together in which it doesn't matter so much what you are doing as long as you are together, in each others' presence.

You can take a minute now and think about which of the love languages you tend to gravitate towards and if there are any that perhaps make you uncomfortable or that you never really thought about as a love language. (There are also online tools, including at 5lovelanguages.com, that can help you identify yours.) This can be a real eye-opener when you look at various relationships through this lens.

I know for me, understanding these love languages has helped transform many of my relationships. My relationship with my father is a perfect example. I realized that my dad's main love language is giving gifts: he is an incredibly generous gift giver. For many years I wished for words of affirmation from him and was constantly disappointed, resentful, and even angry that he never offered them to me. I did not understand that by giving my children and me gifts he was showing his love and appreciation for us.

Once I understood that gift giving was his main love language, I responded to the gifts differently. I felt and showed more gratitude, love, and appreciation for them. This caused him to feel more loved and appreciated by me — a positive snowball effect, in this case. Amazingly, over time it has also led to him actually feeling more comfortable with other love languages. Just recently, he told me that he thinks I am a great mom, a beautiful example of words of affirmation. Even writing this brings tears to my eyes, as it touches my heart so poignantly.

LEARN TO SPEAK LOVE LANGUAGES

For most people, certain love languages can feel challenging and uncomfortable. In my experience, it's most common for people to have a difficult time receiving love in the form of words of affirmation. When you don't grow up receiving love in a particular love language it will often feel foreign and strange. I remember noticing as a teenager that my mom was terrible at receiving compliments. She always deflected them and responded with something negative about herself. For example, a friend might say "Joan, you look beautiful today. What a great sweater that is!" My mom would respond with something along the lines of, "Oh, well. I have to distract you from my terrible haircut."

Interestingly, my mother has shared with me that her mother never called her pretty or beautiful. She would say things like, "You're smart. That's more important than looks." It makes sense that my mother never learned how to receive a compliment because it would have been like trying to comprehend a foreign language to her. Despite desiring words of affirmation from her mother for most of her life, it is not a love language that feels most comfortable for her, either as the receiver or giver.

I have also observed that love languages can have a cultural and generational component to them. I have observed repeatedly in my Jewish family that people very rarely give words of affirmation directly to their loved ones. They may say nice things about the person to other people, but not directly. I remember an old friend of mine who had spent some time with my parents without me there over the years once said, "Your parents are so proud of you." I was flabbergasted. They had never said that to my face but had shared those feelings with my friend.

Another language that can feel uncomfortable to many folks is physical affection. It can feel awkward and uncomfortable when you did not grow up with it. It is also often uncomfortable for people who experienced sexual trauma and/or abuse in their past. This love language was one that I have worked hard over the years to learn to speak.

I remember as a teenager my close friend Lilly was very physically affectionate. We'd be hanging out, sitting on the couch with friends, and she would spontaneously scratch my back or rub my arm. I remember so clearly the feeling that would take over my body in those moments. I was like a rabbit in headlights: frozen with fear, heart and mind racing. My brain would start with, *This is nice! ... Is this nice? I think this is nice. What does she want? Why is she doing this? What am I supposed to do? Am I supposed to rub her back, too? Am I supposed to say something? Say thank you? What? What? What?! Can I move away? She will think that's weird. I can't move away. I'll pretend this feels normal to me.*

I would sit there with a fake frozen grin on my face, my whole body rigid, trying to act normal. For years physical affection made me panic. Even when I became sexually active, I was much more comfortable with sexuality than affection. Somehow, with sex I felt like I knew what I was doing. I knew (or thought I knew) what was expected of me and what the point of it all was. With physical affection, I didn't understand the point, it was a completely foreign practice to me. Over time, using many of the tools I share with you here, I thankfully have been able to change this in my own life. I now feel completely at ease giving and receiving physical affection.

It is also quite common for men and women to speak different love languages. I have seen over and over in couples that a man's love language is acts of service, but his female partner doesn't recognize all the love he is giving her through these acts. This is not true across the board in any way — I myself have tended towards acts of service and gift giving as my most fluent love languages — but sometimes it is helpful to be aware of trends.

In my experience, your main love language usually develops from what you witnessed as a child in the adults around you and which language they most often spoke to you in. Just like with any new language, however, you can learn to speak all of them with ease and fluency. Over time, through building up self-love, practicing presence, choosing compassion for yourself and your loved ones, handling your pain, and seeking pleasure, you will become fluent in all five love languages. This can be a wonderful tool for you to learn to use on your journey towards healthy, joyful, sustainable relationships in all areas of your life.

23

WHEN YOUR NEEDS ARE NOT MET

Another incredibly important truth to acknowledge in order to have healthy, joyful, sustainable relationships is that you will not always receive the love, support, and compassion that you desire in the way that you desire it. That can be disappointing, painful, and depressing, and your protectors may jump into gear and make you angry at someone or something. How can you handle this?

I teach my clients to always start with a self-inquiry process in a situation in which they feel like they are not getting their needs met by a loved one. You begin by asking yourself, *Do I know myself what I desire in this situation?* And then, *What is underneath that desire?*

Why it is so important to ask these questions? They may seem obvious, but take a moment to sit with them. Do you always know exactly what you desire in a situation? I know I often don't. When I feel upset or triggered or embarrassed or any other uncomfortable emotion, chances are good that I am not fully aware of my own desires, of what will make me feel better in the moment. But I still often expect my loved ones to know and provide it for me!

When you can stop and ask the two previous questions before you attempt to communicate those needs to anyone else, you set yourself up way better to being heard and understood and actually getting what you need.

Giving yourself a moment to ask *What is underneath this desire?* is an incredible gift. A little spoiler alert here: it's generally true that no matter what you are asking for, what you desire from a loved one in a particular moment, the deeper need is almost always to feel seen, heard, loved, and/or safe.

Let's look at an example of a recent argument I had with my boyfriend. He had been hurt by a flippant, thoughtless comment I made to him earlier in the week. We had been discussing it for what felt like quite a while, with him explaining why it had hurt him so deeply. I apologized, but I also began to feel very uncomfortable. My body felt squirmy, my heart was pounding, and I could feel the energy in my legs that was telling me to flee the scene immediately. I wanted him to stop talking about how much my words had hurt him. He saw my discomfort and asked me what was wrong. I took a moment to ask myself what was underneath my desire for him to stop talking in that moment. I realized that I was feeling ashamed of myself for the flippant, thoughtless comment from the previous day. The feeling of shame was attached to a story in my head that I was a bad girlfriend and a bad person. I was feeling fear, afraid that he didn't love me anymore and our relationship was over.

Thankfully, I gave myself a moment to connect with my deeper truth and realized that in that moment, I needed to physically connect with him in order to feel safe and loved again. I was able to ask him for a hug. We stood there in his kitchen, just holding each other and breathing together for a few moments. I came back to my center and was able to hold space for him to share his feelings and receive my acknowledgement, apology, and affection.

After getting clear on what you truly desire in a situation and what is underneath that desire, the next step in the self-inquiry process is to ask yourself, *Did I ask him/her for what I needed or desired?* It's amazing how often people expect their loved ones to read their minds and "just know" what they want or need in a situation. This perhaps is another unfortunate result of fairy tale conditioning. You never see a princess and her prince charming communicating their needs and desires to each other. People are complicated; the more you can stay open and present with loved ones and stay in the vulnerable state of communicating honestly and verbally what you need, the more likely you are to get those needs fulfilled. If the only change you make in your relationships is not assuming that other people can read your mind, your relationships will be way more joyful and healthy!

The next question you must ask yourself is, *Did I ask for it in a way that the person understands exactly why I desire what I am asking for?* This takes your communication skills to a deeper level. We all tend to assume that the people we love think, act, and express themselves similarly to how we do (refer back to the love languages section). It's just human nature, I believe, to assume other people are like us, until shown differently.

The incredible work of Alison Armstrong provides information and help in understanding about how men and women, in general, differ in how they express their needs and desires. Armstrong teaches us to recognize and appreciate the love language of the opposite sex. This is helpful even if you are not straight-identifying and only have romantic relationships with people of the same gender as you. One main character in her book, *Keys to the Kingdom*, is a female elementary school teacher who uses these communication tools to understand, appreciate, and communicate better with her male students. The teacher experiences an "A-ha!" moment with one of her young students, named Casey, who was alternatively sullen and disruptive in class. For months she had responded to this by either ignoring his behavior or disciplining him. One day, remembering her recent understanding that boys and men, in general, appreciate feeling needed and helpful she asked him to stay after class: "Would you help me carry some boxes to the storage room?" Without her asking, he made repeated trips back to the classroom, returning with more boxes. She thanked him and commented on his strength. She noticed over the next few days that Casey repeatedly stayed after class and shyly asked her if she needed help with anything else. His behavior during class shifted as well, becoming more attentive and focused on the lessons.

One powerful message that I learned is that boys and men, in general, need to know the reason for doing something for a loved one. They have a deep desire to provide for their loved ones and a deep desire to be appreciated for what they do. Armstrong says, "To a man, nothing is worth doing. Everything is worth providing." Often women do not understand this.

I love her example of a wife wishing her husband would remember to take out the garbage when it was full without her reminding him over and over. The wife feels increasing amounts of frustration and anger throughout the years of her relationship with her husband. She often finds herself asking him in a nagging or sarcastic way to take the garbage out. This causes him to feel less and less appreciated building up his resentment and frustration.

Finally, the couple sit down together to discuss the garbage issue. Using the information and tools that she learned about men's communication styles, the wife asks her husband if she can explain to him what him taking the garbage out means to her. He agrees. She explains that when he takes the garbage out it, she feels cared for. It makes her feel more relaxed and feminine when she can avoid a smelly job that would get her hands dirty. When he takes care of that for her, she feels loved and appreciated by her husband. Her husband's reaction is incredulous: "Taking out the garbage provides all that for you?!" Unsurprisingly, the husband never imagined that his wife equated that chore with so much meaning. Once she explained it to him, though, he was more than happy to do it.

In order to achieve this deeper level of communication and understanding and come to a more joyful, harmonious conclusion, the wife had to go through the above self-inquiry. She did not know previously why she cared so much about her husband failing to take the garbage out. She had to go through the steps of asking herself, *Do I know myself what I desire in this situation?* and then, *What is underneath that desire?*

Prior to that she saw the issue in one of two ways. Either her thought process was something like, *What is wrong with me? I am a terrible wife. I should just take care of the garbage myself. I should just get over this already!* Or it went something along the lines of, *What is wrong with him? He is a terrible husband. So forgetful and blind! He obviously doesn't care about me or the house.* Obviously, neither of these is the truth of the situation, but both are lines of thought that will seem achingly familiar to most of us who have ever cohabitated with another human.

Through self-inquiry the wife in our story realized that the deeper desire associated with the need for her husband to take out the garbage was to feel loved and appreciated by him. Then she could ask herself, *Did I ask him for what I needed or desired?* and *Did I ask for it in a way that he understands why I desire what I am asking for?*

She realized that yes, she had asked him to take the garbage out. She perhaps realized that she had asked him many years earlier but that lately it had been less of an ask and more of an irritated or snarky demand. She then realized that she had never talked to him about why it was important to her. Subsequently, she was able to approach him to have a conversation about the garbage from a completely different perspective, with a radically different intention and tone. She remembered her love for him and that he loved her and wanted to do things for her that made her life easier and made her feel good.

24

WHEN A LOVED ONE CANNOT MEET YOUR NEEDS

So, there you are, across the kitchen table from a loved one. You have just gone through the process of asking *Do I know myself what I desire in this situation?* The answer is a clear yes. You have clarity on what is underneath that desire and it is some variation on needing to feel loved, appreciated, and safe. You then ask your loved one for what you desire in a way that they understand clearly. And the answer is no, they can't give you what you need. What do you do then?

The first important step is to differentiate between a small no and a big no. Say you ask, "Can we talk about how nervous I am for our upcoming Thanksgiving dinner — the first one since my aunt died?" An example of a small no could be something like your partner saying, "No, I can't talk about that with you right now. I would be happy to talk with you about it tonight, after the kids go to bed." Perhaps you had asked your partner when she is about to leave for work or heading out to meet a friend. This is an example of a small no, not because it's unimportant but because although your partner did not say yes in the moment, the no is just temporary.

But what if you ask the same question and your partner responds with, "I can't talk about this with you. You always want to talk about your feelings about your aunt's death and I just can't anymore. I am mourning my own father's death and I just don't have the emotional wherewithal to support you through your grief. I'm sorry, babe."

In this example, your partner has a completely valid reason for not being able to give you what you need, right? So, what do you do?

I chose this example specifically because there are no bad guys in this scenario. Both people are grieving and suffering and in need of extra support and love. Life happens and no matter how conscious and healthy your relationship is, there will be times when you feel that reality is continually smacking you in the face.

In these cases, you can turn again to another type of self-inquiry process, this time to help you understand how to handle the difficult situation of not getting your desires met in a way that you feel you need. If we stay with the previous example of wanting your partner to talk with you to soothe your anxiety and grief, begin by asking yourself, *Can I fill this need myself?*

Can you hold yourself in this grieving process? Can you soothe your own nervous system through self-love, meditation, prayer, or any of your other self-love tools? If the answer is yes, super! You can then take care of yourself in that moment from a place of gratitude that you have the ability, tools, and knowledge to care for yourself so well instead of from a place of resentment that your partner couldn't provide it for you.

If the answer is no, then ask yourself, *Can I get this need met by another loved one?* Is there another person you can talk to about your grief for your aunt and your nervousness about Thanksgiving? If the answer is yes, great! Reach out to this other person, receive love and support there, and come back to your partnership with your emotional cup filled up.

What if the answer to the above is no? What if, after the previous inquiry, you realize that you really need your partner's support in this situation and nothing else will help you feel safe and loved and peaceful except a discussion with her? The only thing to do in that situation then is to acknowledge the truth and allow yourself to feel what comes up — most likely a mix of sadness, disappointment, rejection, and loneliness. Allow yourself to feel these feelings without creating and attaching meanings to them. The feelings do not mean, for instance, that your partner does not love you. They do not mean that you are not worthy or deserving of love. They do not mean that your partner is a bad person.

Don't allow yourself to judge the past differently or project into the future. The only truths here are that your partner was not able to meet your needs in this specific way, at this specific time, and that you feel sad and disappointed about it.

Now this is the tree-level view. Keeping your focus on this particular situation is necessary to allow yourself to feel the uncomfortable feelings and hold yourself through them. Allow those hurt feelings to move freely through you without blocking, numbing, or judging them.

When you come back to a place of calm and centeredness, you can switch to the forest-level view again. That is, you also need to periodically look at longer overall patterns in your relationship. Has your partner been unable to support you before? How often? Can you look with clear eyes at your history with this person and really see if you get your needs met more often than not? Which needs do you regularly get met by this person? Are there needs that you most often do not get met? How important is it to you that you get these needs met by this person? [9]Difficult truths sometimes need to be addressed at these moments. If you realize that most of your core crucial needs are not being met by the person you need them to be met by, then you will need to change your

---

[9] Check out the exercise called "Write Your List." Pay particular attention to the section called "deal breakers."

relationship with that person in some way. As difficult as it is, avoiding this truth only leads to less joy and ease in both of your futures.

Of course it feels bad to not get what you need from someone you love, but being asked to provide something to someone you love that you are unable to give also feels awful. I experienced this painful truth with an ex-boyfriend, Kevin, whom I loved very much. He repeatedly expressed a desire to spend more time with me. He felt angry and hurt when I would tell him that I could not meet this need because of my family and work situation. I would have loved to spend more time with him, but I was unable to. I eventually ended the relationship. We both experienced pain and heartache afterwards, but it was necessary so that Kevin could eventually have a relationship that met his needs and I could have a relationship that met mine.

The above scenario might have gone a different way, too. Perhaps Kevin could have done a self-inquiry and realized what was underneath his feeling that he needed to spend more time with me was a need for connection and belonging. Then we could have stayed together while he focused on deepening his connection to himself. Or perhaps he could have focused on creating and building up more of his friendships to meet his need for more connection and belonging in his life.

I believe there wasn't a right or wrong choice in the above situation, nor in most situations involving love and relationships. As long as you are living in alignment with your integrity, taking responsibility for your feelings, practicing presence and compassion, and speaking your truth, there are no "bad guys." When you strive to accept reality as truth, allow yourself to feel your feelings in reaction to that, reality and take everything as an opportunity to deepen and expand your loving connection to yourself and others, you will experience way more peace, joy, and love in all your relationships.

CONCLUSION

My intention in writing this book is to help you feel confident that you can have healthy, joyful relationships with everyone in your life. I want you to know deep in your bones that you can break free from the old, worn-out patterns in relationships that you have been stuck in for as long as you can remember. I want you to lay down the sword you have been wielding against yourself in the form of self-judgment and criticism and build your daily practice of checking in with yourself with presence and compassion. You begin your journey towards healthy, joyful relationships by taking the first step towards complete acceptance, trust, and love in yourself, including all your resistance, challenging emotions, and protector parts, using the tools I share here. From there, you continue on your step-by-step path by applying the same tools, utilizing all the knowledge and wisdom you gained through your internal work to fill all the relationships in your life with more joy, pleasure, and love.

You take everything you learn about how to be present with yourself, how to strengthen the trust, acceptance, and love that you have in your relationship with yourself, and then you walk it outwards into all areas of your life — especially to all the people you have chosen to have intimate relationships with. When you hold space for people in your life, you create possibilities for honest communication and authentic connection. This is how you build an honest, real foundation in every relationship. The need to be seen, heard, and appreciated is basic and universal in every human relationship.

Just as you need to hold space for your loved ones to be their authentic selves, so too do you have to show up as your authentic, vulnerable self. You have to voice your needs, your fears, and your heart's desires. You need to speak your truth even if it may cause a loved one pain, and you need to let go of the illusion that you can control another person's path in life.

You also need to let go of the fairy tale illusion that the majority of us have been conditioned to believe in. I ask you to both recognize that having attachments to other people, — choosing close, loving relationships — means choosing pain and heartache sometimes and also that you can choose to have more pleasure in your daily life by focusing on filling up your pleasure treasure chest. When you allow yourself to feel, deep in your bones, that you deserve joy and that you are worthy of pleasure, you are better able to weather life's storms and more easily remember that pleasure and joy always come back into your life. You can begin quite simply by asking yourself throughout your day, *How could this be pleasurable?* You can also commit to a regular self love meditation or practice.

And again, just as with learning to trust and accept yourself first and then walking that outwards, you can do the same thing with love and pleasure. Practice gratitude for all the people in your life that you get to love each day. Show them your love. Learn to see, hear, and appreciate your loved ones' languages of love. Choose compassion. Choose kindness. Choose thoughtfulness.

Do your best to remember in the hardest moments that you love them. Learn how to communicate your love and your needs and desires. Do a self inquiry process when you feel unloved, unappreciated, or angry with a loved one.

Please remember that choosing compassion, kindness, and love is just that. It does not mean anything else about what sort of relationship you have with a particular person. With

CONCLUSION

certain people in your life, choosing compassion, love, and kindness for yourself as well as for them may mean physically distancing yourself from them. If you love someone who is a drug addict, for instance, who refuses to admit it much less seek help, there is very little you can do for them by staying active in their lives except enable their addiction. But you can always love them and offer support for them whenever they are ready to receive it.

I encourage you to take this guidance and these tools and use them in every area of your life, not just relationships with people. As I said in the introduction, I have used these same tools to help people transform one of the most important relationships in all our lives, that with food, as well as supporting people to heal from dysfunctional relationships with their businesses and careers.

Try the exercises and practices and reach out for support in the Facebook group (http://bit.ly/ChooseLovetheBook). You are not alone. You are loved and you deserve to have happy, healthy, sustainable relationships in your life.

SELF-GROWTH EXERCISES

These exercises are listed in the order they are discussed in the main body of *Choose Love*. Use them in the way that works for you. Your choice to read this book started you towards your goal of building healthy, joyful relationships with everyone in your life. Engaging with these meditations, practices and exercises is the crucial next stage of the journey. All of the audio meditations can be found at Margot's MemberVault site here, along with additional content: https://margotschulman.vipmembervault.com/teaser

Section One

1. Checking in Tool
2. Breaking the Trigger Pattern
3. Somatic Practice of Bridging Love to Fear
4. Write Your List
5. Practice Holding Space with Children
6. Remembering Your Choices
7. Thich Nhat Hanh's "No earache today!"
8. Investigate Red Flags

Section Two

1. Presence with Pain
2. Shoring Up Inner Strength and Wisdom

Section Three

1. Pleasure-Seeking Practice
2. Investigate your Relationship with Pleasure
3. Gratitude Practice
4. Pleasure Treasure Chest Practice
5. Self-Love Meditation
6. Somatic Self-Massage Practice
7. Recognizing Evidence of Love
8. Release from Judgment — Internally and Externally
9. Change the Stories
10. Love Languages Quiz
11. Self-Inquiry Process

PART ONE EXERCISES: PRACTICE PRESENCE & BUILD ACCEPTANCE

1. CHECKING IN TOOL

With practice, this tool will become so familiar to you that you will do it without thinking. It is the first step in creating acceptance and building trust within yourself. An easy way to begin this is to commit to doing it at certain times throughout your day. For instance, I often do it when sitting in my car at a red light. You could choose when you are on the bus or train or brushing your teeth, etc. Simply ask yourself: *What sensations are present in my body right now? What thoughts are circling in my brain? What emotions am I feeling at this moment?* The goal is to gather information, getting to know yourself without judgment or labels.

2. Breaking the Trigger Pattern

This practice helps you bring awareness to your triggers. This creates space to change your actions and reactions. You can even practice this in conjunction with the previous exercise. When, after checking in with yourself, you notice that you feel tension, stress, anxiety, fear, shame, or anger do the following:

1. Stop whatever you are doing or saying.
2. Take a breath and start counting in your head. Focus on counting and breathing.
3. Count until you feel yourself come back to calmness.
4. Focus your awareness on the physical sensations present in your body. Notice the thoughts that are present in your mind.
5. Do nothing else, say nothing else, until you feel calm and centered again.

3. Somatic Practice of Connecting Love to Fear

This practice goes deeper into healing your trigger patterns. Use this practice to heal unhealthy relationship patterns. It builds up your ability to feel completely safe and loved inside, no matter what is happening around you.
https://www.dropbox.com/s/hwjoxgp2mwkvpxu/Love%20and%20Fear%20Meditation.wav?dl=0

4. Write Your List

This exercise will help you learn more about yourself in relation to other people. You get clear on exactly what you need and want in all relationships. A few things to note: First of all, this list is not written in stone; it's meant to be checked and changed often. Lots of dating coaches have versions of the list. I use it with my clients and have used it myself over the years. You can pick any version you like or use mine; I don't see too much of a difference. Please pay close attention to the part of the list labeled "deal breakers." This is the part of the list that will most help you stay present and focused on reality. Also feel free to use this exercise with everyone in your life, not just romantic partners.

    a. List your "Must Haves" in a relationship — everything that you need in order to have a healthy, joyful relationship with someone.
    b. List your "Cherries on Top" — everything that you would love to have in this relationship.
    c. List all the amazing qualities that **you** bring to a relationship.
    d. List your "Deal Breakers" — things your partner cannot do or be in order for your relationship to work.

Example of a list about friendship: I must trust that my friend genuinely respects me and will be honest with me about important matters. A "cherry on top" would be if she had a similar schedule as mine and we could hang out at least once a month! I am extremely supportive to all my friends and a lot of fun to spend time with. A "deal breaker" for me in friendship is someone who is committed to identifying as a martyr.

5. Practice Holding Space with Children

This practice helps you build more acceptance and trust into your relationship with your children.

    a. One way to do this is by going around the dinner table each night and asking your family members to each share one thing they are proud of themselves for, one thing they failed at that day (or would like to do better another time, if you don't like using the word *fail*), and one emotion they are experiencing in that moment. Pay attention to your reactions when your family members are sharing. Notice if your mind wanders or you tend to start thinking of responses immediately. Use it like a mediation: when you notice your mind wandering, do not judge or criticize yourself, just bring your attention back to the person speaking.

b. Another way to do this is to take a few minutes at the end of each day to write down which activities, attitudes, or words from your kids triggered you that day to behave in a way that you later regretted. Pick one example from your list, close your eyes, and put yourself back in that moment. Ask yourself: *What story did I hear in that moment?* Take a few moments to write down what comes up. When you have done this a few times, notice what stories or thoughts are recurrent. Then ask yourself: *What is a different story I can tell myself about these moments?*

6. Remembering Your Choices

This exercise helps you move through a moment of frustration with your children and come back more easily to feelings of love and gratitude. Ask yourself simply: *What choices have I made that brought me to this moment and this experience?*

7. Thich Nhat Hanh's "No earache today!"

This practice builds your capacity for experiencing joy throughout your everyday life. Refocus your mind on what you can feel gratitude for in a moment, no matter how silly or simple it seems.

a. Ask yourself: *What does not hurt in my body right now?*

b. Ask yourself: *What do I have that other folks in the world do not have — clean water? a warm bed? people who love me? the ability to walk and see and hear? and so on.*

8. Red Flags

This exercise helps you learn to make different choices in relationships by examining past relationships.

a. Pick a particular relationship from your past that you remember specifics about. It can help to do this with an old friend who may see your red flags more easily than you do.
b. Spend at least 10 minutes examining this relationship like an anthropologist, looking for any and all clues that in hindsight can help uncover the bigger story of your oldest, deepest, negative neurological patterns.
c. Notice when you felt fear of not being accepted and loved in that relationship.
d. Notice what the other person was doing or saying in those moments that triggered you into a state of fear or anxiety.

Part Two Exercises: Expand Compassion & Trust

1. Presence with Pain

This exercise is the crucial first step in shifting your relationship with emotional pain. You begin to gently question your previous interpretations of painful sensations and emotions.

a. Remember a situation in which you felt heartbroken such as hearing a song on the radio that reminds you of a lost lover.

b. Notice the sensations in your body: Is there heaviness in your chest? Constriction in your throat? A roiling in your belly?
   c. Now notice what stories are getting triggered in your mind.
   d. Ask yourself *Do I know with 100% certainty that that story is the truth? Is there another story that may possibly have some truth as well?*
   e. Bring your awareness back to your breathing and the present moment you are in - safe and quiet.

2. Shoring Up Inner Strength and Wisdom

This meditation will be helpful to do regularly throughout your self-healing journey. It will support you by increasing your ability to access a feeling of strength and security in your body whenever you need it. It can be done seated or reclining and is approximately 10 minutes long. https://www.dropbox.com/s/w4p9421w2df2dm7/Strength_Meditation.m4a?dl=0

Part Three Exercises: Pursue Pleasure, Choose Love

1. Pleasure-Seeking Practice

This practice is best done every day! It's especially important to balance yourself when you are regularly doing a lot of heavy emotional work.

   a. Begin by simply asking yourself, "How could this be pleasurable?" at various points throughout your normal day — in traffic, waiting at a doctor's office, doing mindless paperwork at your job, changing a diaper.

b. Eventually challenge yourself with how far you can go with this. Can you bring some fun and lightness to the most dreaded part of your regular routine?

2. Investigate your Relationship with Pleasure

This exercise is helpful if you find yourself quite resistant to the above practice. Spend 10 minutes journaling about your feelings and thoughts about pleasure. Ask yourself questions like:

a. What did your parents teach you about pleasure and joy?
b. What does your religion teach you about pleasure?
c. Were you ever shamed, scolded, or punished as a child for playing, or having innocent fun?

3. Gratitude Practice

This practice is simple and incredibly powerful. When practiced regularly, it will fill your life and your relationships with more joy and pleasure — guaranteed! Feeling gratitude is like a muscle: the more you use it, the stronger it gets and the easier it becomes to perform the exercise. It is okay to feel weird about this at first; most skills feel weird when you are first learning them.

a. List things you feel grateful for in that moment.
b. This can be done through journaling or speaking out loud. (I like to do it before going to sleep every night. I just speak out loud whatever comes to mind in the moment that I am grateful for that day.)

SELF-GROWTH EXERCISES

4. Pleasure Treasure Chest Practice

Embrace the concept of a Pleasure Treasure Chest as an important part of your regular self-care practice. It helps you build your strength, resiliency, and empowerment in all your relationships.

   a. Spend a few minutes every day writing a list of things that make you feel happy.
   b. Add to this whenever you remember to.
   c. If you feel resistance, do not judge or criticize yourself. Notice what your reactions are telling you about you and your relationship to pleasure and joy. You might also go back to the "Investigate Your Relationship with Pleasure" exercise.

5. Self Love Meditation

Self-love practices are necessary throughout all times in your life but are especially crucial now as you ascend out of the muddy ruts of old relationship patterning. This is an easy to follow meditation in which you work with somatic tools to fill your heart up with more love. It is seven minutes long. https://www.dropbox.com/s/8m5hbygkb8kohet/Heart%20Meditationv3-1.wav?dl=0.

6. Somatic Self-Massage Practice

You can think of this as an active form of meditation. You love yourself with your own physical touch. Allow at least 20 minutes for these.

   a. Find the link for a breast massage here: https://www.dropbox.com/s/qrw864e5s80sa71/Breast%20Massage.wav?dl=0

b. Find the link for testicle massage here: *https://www.dropbox.com/s/6gep5d62152m6r8/Testicle%20Massage.m4a?dl=0*

7. Recognizing Physical Evidence of Love

Use this simple exercise whenever your feelings for a particular person feel complicated, confusing or overwhelming. Remember: the goal of this exercise is not to shift anything happening inside you. Just build awareness and practice paying close attention to your internal feelings and thoughts in a moment. Take a few minutes at the end of the second round to just sit and notice what came up for you, what you felt during the exercise. You can also spend a few minutes writing about it if that helps you process the information.

1. Get situated in a quiet private space. You can sit, stand, or lie down for this meditation exercise.
2. Set a timer for 20 minutes.
3. Close your eyes and allow your internal focus to rest on your breathing for a few moments. You are breathing normally here, not changing anything, just noticing your breath, in and out of your body.
4. Invite your mind to bring up a picture of a person in your life whom you love dearly and without question. See them in front of you, a few feet away.
5. If they are not already looking at you, picture them turning towards you and opening their arms out wide, inviting you in for a hug.
6. Now let your internal awareness scan your entire body, face, and mind, paying very close attention to the sensations that are present and the words that run through your mind.
7. Speak them out loud to yourself. Allow yourself as much time as feels good for this part.

8. When that feels complete, invite your mind to bring up a picture of a person in your life who you feel conflicted or confusing emotions about. See them in front of you, a few feet away.
9. If they are not already looking at you, picture them turning towards you and opening their arms out wide, inviting you in for a hug.
10. Once again, let your internal awareness scan your entire body, face, and mind, paying very close attention to the sensations that are present and the words that run through your mind.
11. Speak them out loud to yourself.
12. Allow your awareness to come back to your breathing at any time that you need.

8. Release from Judgment — Internally and Externally

This practice is useful when you often find yourself mentally criticizing yourself and/or labeling someone in your life as "evil" or "bad."

a. Ask yourself: *What if my best friend was relating this situation to me? Would I berate her/him for their feelings? Or would I feel compassion and offer them support and love and perhaps a reminder that they are doing the best they can?*
b. Ask yourself: *Is it possible that this person that I am so angry at is doing the best they can, given their wounding, pain, and negative patterns?*

9. Change the Stories

This practice is incredible for increasing your ability to feel joyful, peaceful, and grateful in all your close relationships.

Practice first with lighter situations. With time, focus, and practice, you can start to shift the stories, the sensations of heavier emotions and situations.

   a. Think about a recent painful emotional experience. What is the first story that comes to mind? Write it down.
   b. Ask yourself if you can you rewrite that story to include any natural feelings of gratitude and joy. Then write down that new story.

An example from my life: Every Thanksgiving my Aunt Sherri and I would spend the day cooking side by side, sharing our love of food, laughing, and drinking her famous Manhattans. She passed away two months before this year's celebration, so I had a choice. I could either think about how tragic it was that we had to do Thanksgiving without her and how sad my children would be, or I could think of the upcoming Thanksgiving dinner as a celebration in her honor. Every dish I cooked, every laugh I had with another relative, would be a toast to her memory. Did it keep me from feeling sad? No. But it allowed me to experience feelings of joy, gratitude, and love as well.

10. Love Languages Quiz

You can find more info about the love languages on the author's website. Spend some time exploring this idea through journaling or in conversation with loved ones. Which love languages are you most fluent in? Which do you find challenging? How about your partner, parents, etc.?

Here is a link to a quiz if you have trouble figuring out which are your most fluent love languages: https://www.5lovelanguages.com/quizzes/

11. SELF-INQUIRY PROCESS WITH DESIRES

Recall a recent situation in your life in which you felt that your needs were not met with a loved one. Journal your answers to these questions about that situation:

1. Do I know, myself, what I desire in this situation?
2. What is underneath that desire?
3. Did I ask him/her for what I needed or desired?
4. Did I ask for it in a way that the person understands why I desire what I am asking for?

Example of a Pleasure Treasure List
(This is incomplete and meant only to provide a little inspiration.)

- All things Harry Potter — reading the books alone, reading the books with my kids, visiting Universal Studios, watching the films
- Snuggling myself up in my super soft blanket
- Drinking coffee on my back porch and looking at the incredible colors on the trees
- Making my kids laugh by acting silly or goofy
- Dancing around my kitchen
- Doing headstands
- Bouncing at the local trampoline gym
- Rocking out to 80's hits while walking on a local hiking trail
- Holding babies
- Sitting with my toes in sand
- Being in any kind of water — ocean, lake, creek, shower, hot tub, or bath
- Walking through produce markets in other countries
- Coloring with brightly colored markers
- Listening to my daughter practice piano

- Playing basketball with my son
- Watching my kids playing together and cracking each other up
- Supporting a friend through a difficult situation
- Building a good fire in my wood stove
- Mowing my lawn
- Growing veggies in my garden
- Picking flowers at a local farm
- Making fresh ricotta cheese
- Making chocolates

ABOUT THE AUTHOR

Margot Schulman is a Master Level Love, Relationship and Life Coach. She specializes in guiding men and women to deepen the acceptance and trust in their relationship with themselves and then gracefully expand that solid foundation into exponentially greater joy, passion and love in all their close relationships.

Her mission is to help people break free from old, stuck negative patterns in order to stay outrageously empowered, joyful, self-loving and free in all parts of their life!

When she is not coaching, teaching or writing, she can be found dancing; giggling with her children; connecting to Divine Mama Earth; or cooking and eating delicious food with her beloved Danny.

Connect with her in the Interwebs here:

Margot@mindfulbadasscoaching.com

www.mindfulbadasscoaching.com

https://margotschulman.vipmembervault.com/teaser

Instagram https://www.instagram.com/a_mindfulbadass/?hl=en

Facebook https://www.facebook.com/mindfulbadasscoaching/

And
http://bit.ly/ChooseLovetheBook

www.ingramcontent.com/pod-product-compliance
Lightning Source LLC
LaVergne TN
LVHW041637060526
838200LV00040B/1603